D1035423

The Tale of Kieu

by Nguyen Du

TRANSLATED AND ANNOTATED

by Huynh Sanh Thong

*with a Preface by Gloria Emerson
and The Historical Background
by Alexander Woodside*

*VINTAGE BOOKS
A DIVISION OF RANDOM HOUSE
NEW YORK*

PL
4378.9
.N5
K513
1973b
895.922 N5

Nguyễn, Du

The tale of Kieu.

DABNEY LANCASTER LIBRARY
LONGWOOD COLLEGE
FARMVILLE, VIRGINIA 23901

VINTAGE BOOKS EDITION October 1973
First Edition
Copyright © 1973 by Huynh Sanh Thong (translator)
Introduction and Preface Copyright © 1973 by Random House, Inc.
All rights reserved under International and Pan-American Copyright Conventions.
Published in the United States by Random House, Inc., New York; and
simultaneously in Canada by Random House of Canada Limited, Toronto.

Library of Congress Cataloging in Publication Data

Nguyễn Du, 1765–1820.
  The tale of Kieu.

  Translation of Kim-Vân-Kiêu.
  Bibliography: p.
  I. Huỳnh Sanh Thông, tr. II. Title.
[PL4378.9.N5K513 1973b]   895.9'2'212   73–4735
ISBN 0–394–71925–5 (pbk.)

Manufactured in the United States of America

100646

This translation is for Yen

76-04478

Preface
by Gloria Emerson

So much has been written by Americans about the Vietnamese when it was too difficult for us to say good morning to them in their own language, or scan a newspaper, or even ask a child his age. We wrote and wrote on how they looked, and what they most longed for, and what they had lost. We wrote about their food, their fortune tellers and their funerals, how they fought and how they fell back.

But we were illiterates in Vietnam.

Moving through the villages, asking people over and over again to describe their misfortunes, I learned of this poem— almost too light a word to describe *Kim Van Kieu*—which has no moral equivalent in English. In a village (whose name I have long forgotten) there was an elderly man who recited lines from *Kim Van Kieu*, and I, impatient and unable to understand a single sound he was making, thought this was a gentle lunatic singing in the sun. For what American could ever imagine one of us in Broken Bone, Nebraska, or in any of our villages, reciting aloud to a visitor: "When in disgrace with fortune and men's eyes. . . ." Who remembers five, ten of Shakespeare's sonnets?

But the Vietnamese remember hundreds of lines from *Kim Van Kieu*, so deeply are the words, and what they mean, etched within them. Perhaps memory, but only that, has not been ruined or weakened by the war.

Once I even saw two Vietnamese schoolgirls tell their fortunes by opening a copy of *Kim Van Kieu* to see what passage to read.

Long after I came to Saigon, a Vietnamese actually smiled at me, and looked pleased and spoke first. He was a customs inspector at Tan Son Nhut airport in Saigon. He saw a copy of *Kim Van Kieu* in my suitcase.

"You know it?" he asked me in English. I said I hoped to, and it made him smile.

In Vietnam, I learned of Thuy Kieu and began, at last, to understand what I had not yet understood: how the Vietnamese perceive suffering and sacrifice and sorrow, and why so very many of them are able to bear so much of it.

One night, quite by chance, I asked my interpreter Nguyen Ngoc Luong the meaning of a line in *Kim Van Kieu*. I must have asked him for meanings of one kind or another at least twenty times a day, and it often made him very tired indeed. But that night he laughed and began to recite the opening lines of the great poem. His was not the only voice. There was a night messenger at the *New York Times* office in Saigon who knew all about losing and what war teaches us. We called him the Capitaine and he always wore the thin, old jacket of his dead son who had been a soldier. He began to recite *Kim Van Kieu*, and still a third man, a Vietnamese named Dinh whose specialty was politics, came into that room, and the three of them together went on reciting.

For a little while that night, there was something in their faces I had never seen before and now, in another country and so much later, I can still remember how they looked.

The Historical Background
by Alexander Woodside

All students of East Asian and Southeast Asian history and civilization will be profoundly grateful to Huynh Sanh Thong for giving English-speaking peoples, at last, such a shrewd and fastidious translation of one of the masterpieces of traditional Asian literature. To the Vietnamese people themselves, *The Tale of Kieu* is much more than just a glorious heirloom from their literary past. It has become a kind of continuing emotional laboratory in which all the great and timeless issues of personal morality and political obligation are tested and resolved (or left unresolved) for each new generation. Western readers who are curious about Vietnam and the Vietnamese may well gain more real wisdom from cultivating a discriminating appreciation of this one poem than they will from reading the entire library of scholarly and journalistic writings upon modern Vietnam which has accumulated in the West in the past decade. As a vivid transcript of Vietnamese approaches to the dilemmas of the human condition, *The Tale of Kieu* has survived in, and gained new strength from, hundreds of different contexts. But what was the historical setting in which it was actually created?

At the beginning of the nineteenth century, Vietnam was a society of perhaps seven or eight million people. In other words, its population was probably larger than that of the United States at the time of Washington's Farewell Address and almost as large as that of Great Britain, then just beginning to industrialize. Like the Japanese and the Koreans, the Vietnamese people had for many centuries belonged to what might well be called the East Asian classical world: they regarded themselves as the devoted heirs of those traditions of government, philosophy, literature, and moral and social theory which had been developed first in China in the age of the great Chinese philosophers, Confucius and Mencius and others, and then elaborated and changed by hundreds of succeeding generations of Chinese classical scholars. Even Vietnamese Buddhism eventually acquired an East Asian classical complexion. It was the Mahayana Buddhism of China, Korea, and Japan, rather than the Theravada Buddhism of Siam and Burma, and all Vietnamese Buddhist sutras were carefully written in the classical Chinese language. The author of *The Tale of Kieu*, Nguyen Du, who visited China as a Vietnamese ambassador to the Peking court, was a superb East Asian classicist in his own right, and as Mr. Thong so justly observes, *The Tale of Kieu* is a genuine "treasure-trove of classical Chinese learning."

But the false conclusion many Western readers might be inclined to draw from such a summary is that Vietnam was simply a callow imitation, on a much smaller scale, of the Chinese empire. Nothing could have been farther from the truth. Each one of the four traditional East Asian societies had created its own distinct cultural world within the broader framework of the classical civilization to which all paid homage; Vietnamese ruling elites themselves deliberately controlled their cultural borrowing from China, and influences from elsewhere in Southeast Asia were also at work in many important and subtle ways in the march of Vietnamese daily life. To some extent, Nguyen Du's relationship to the East Asian classical world was really somewhat like the relationship of many of his Western literary contemporaries to *their* Greek and Roman classical tradition, and perhaps this observation may be of some help to readers who are baffled by the parade of Chinese allusions in *The Tale of Kieu*. (I hope it is not necessary to comment on the confusion of readers who assume that the lavish use of classical conventions in poetry rules out originality.)

If Nguyen Du makes forty-six references in his poem to the Chinese *Book of Odes* (whose songs date from about the tenth to the seventh century B.C.), much of the form and spirit of his English contemporary Wordsworth's *Ode: Intimations of Immortality from Recollections of Early Childhood* are borrowed from Pindar, the Greek poet of the fifth century B.C. When another one of Nguyen Du's English contemporaries, John Keats, writes about the "dizzy pain" he feels after gazing at the Elgin Marbles in the British Museum, or about the permanent "friend to man" that he finds in a Grecian urn, or about the world of high romance he tastes by looking into Chapman's Homer, he expresses a rapturous adoration of the Greek classical tradition that Vietnamese poets matched, but could hardly transcend, in their admiration of the Chinese classical past.

Going farther, it would not even be very difficult to compare the intense classical atmospheres in which political debates were conducted, and political decisions made, in Vietnam and in Western countries during the lifetime of Nguyen Du. When a Western missionary informed the emperor Gia-long, Nguyen Du's master, that Christianity was 1,815 years old, the statement became intelligible to the Vietnamese court only when Gia-long's official astronomer, Nguyen Huu Than, converted the date of Christianity's genesis to a point in the reign of the Chinese Han Yüan-ti emperor (a rather creative conversion, since Han Yüan-ti had ruled China from 48 to 32 B.C.). Gia-long himself sententiously declared in 1816 that the Chinese Han dynasty (206 B.C.–220 A.D., roughly contemporary with Rome) and not the many dynasties that had come after it exemplified the highest ideals and the most successful patterns of human political behavior. But Gia-long's obeisances to the memory of the Han empire were not remarkably different from Western invocations of the memory of Greece and Rome at about the same time. Political oratory during the French Revolution modeled itself upon Cicero's speeches, and the entire Napoleonic era in France flaunted its Roman symbolism, from political titles to regimental insignia to David's paintings. Even in the young American republic, the Senate took its name from a Roman institution, the names of cities and towns as far apart as Cincinnati, Ohio, and Athens, Georgia, were inspired by talismanic memories from Greek and Roman history, and Thomas Jefferson's Virginia home was built as a proud imitation of a Roman villa.

To a very real degree, then, *The Tale of Kieu* was the product of a world in which the hegemony of classical ideas and ornamentation was still almost as striking in the West as it was in East Asia, not of a world in which the West had completely and irrevocably discarded its classical heritage and East Asia alone remained enclosed in a cocoon of traditionalism.

Moreover, Vietnam was not a completely static society whose institutions were in perfect equilibrium, even if it was not, like Europe, on the verge of dramatic industrial change. The author of *The Tale of Kieu* spent most of the first thirty-five years of his life (1765–1800) attempting to survive the Tay-son revolution. This vast social and political movement began in the south central frontier lands of Binh Dinh province in 1771, demolished all the existing governments of Vietnam with a flamboyant program of "virtuous and charitable banditry" which included some very modest redistributions of upper-class wealth, and attained a brilliant climax with the triumphant defeat of an invading Chinese army in 1788–1789. Nguyen Du was not a supporter of the Tay-sons, and this fact demonstrates the "historical limitations" of his thought in the eyes of some modern Viet-

namese Marxist critics who cherish Du's poetry but also regard
the Tay-son revolution as a miracle of military prowess and of
attempted social emancipation. Impeccably loyal to the Le
dynasty (1427–1788), which the Tay-sons had eventually destroyed, Du spent much of this period as an impoverished back-
woods scholar, haunted by the tragedy of a vanished "orthodox
succession" of emperors to which his family had been deeply
attached, and by the whirlpool of unstable, promiscuous political
affiliations which had replaced it. It can be justly claimed, however, that Du was under very few illusions about the perversions
of bureaucratic government and social morality in Vietnam
which had stimulated the Tay-son movement. His descriptions
of corrupt officials and of dealers in prostitution—and, as Mr.
Thong suggests, the spectral presence of the inspirational leader
of the Tay-sons, Nguyen Hue, in the character Tu Hai—make
this clear.

Du spent the last two decades of his life (1800–1820) consid-
ering, and practicing, an unenthusiastic collaboration with the
new rulers of Vietnam, the Nguyen dynasty. The Nguyen house,
whose roots were in the center and the south rather than in the
north, ultimately repressed the exhausted Tay-son movement
and made a new national capital at Hué in central Vietnam in
1802. Members of the old northern scholar class, of which
Nguyen Du was a member, found it possible to serve the first
Nguyen emperor, Gia-long (1802–1820) because his reign promised peace and unification after nearly three centuries of dis-
guised and undisguised political divisions and because the
Nguyen dynasty itself had not directly caused the downfall of
their deeply mourned Le monarchy. Their cooperation, however, often concealed an inner havoc of melancholy self-recrimi-
nation, resentment of the misfortunes of the past, and doubts
about the future.

They knew that Gia-long did not depend entirely upon them:
his power had also been augmented by the assistance of several

hundred French engineers and soldiers of fortune. These exotic private servants of the new emperor designed imposing walled citadels for him on the sites of many provincial towns and also at Hué. But what one of Gia-long's senior officials called, in 1804, the "sighs and grievances" of the luckless Vietnamese peasants who were forced to build the walls of Hué suggested that the dynasty was fatally widening the gulf between itself and ordinary Vietnamese society at a time when a shattering military confrontation with the West was less than sixty years away. Nguyen Du, of course, did not have any premonition of this coming confrontation. He could hardly have been oblivious, however, to recurrent storm signals from the countryside: some 105 discernible peasant uprisings have been counted for the brief eighteen years of Gia-long's reign, including eighteen, or one per year, in just one province (Quang Ngai) and a Triad Society insurrection in the north in the year 1807. It was against this background—the reluctant superimposition of a loyalty of convenience upon the memory of a true loyalty buried in the past, combined with an apprehensive consciousness of continuing social unrest despite the country's formal reunification—that Nguyen Du wrote *Kieu*.

It should be added that Nguyen Du never enjoyed real political power of any kind after 1802, despite his formidable erudition and his nominal adherence to the political causes of Gia-long's empire. His official court biography, compiled in the nineteenth century, tells us that he served as a provincial prefect but resigned this post because of "illness," that he was summoned to Hué in 1806 to serve in one of the imperial "scholars' pavilions," that he became a provincial registrar in 1809, that he served as an envoy on a Vietnamese tribute mission to China in 1813, that he was promoted for these services to the position of vice-president of the Hué Board of Rites, and that he died in 1820 as he was about to depart on another mission to China. But the Hué scholars' pavilions were usually little more than airless, nonpolitical sanctuaries which collected and employed elderly Le dynasty scholars or supplied learned tutors to the children of the imperial family. Diplomatic missions to China, for their part, were customarily staffed with poetic masters of Chinese literature who could demonstrate the high degree of civilization of Vietnamese politics in unimpeachably Chinese terms when they entered the frigidly condescending atmospheres of Peking audience halls.

Real power in Vietnam, almost to the time of Du's death, was awarded to the military paladins of the "Bangkok honor roll," to those homespun soldiers from central and southern Vietnam with uneven educations who had endured exile with Gia-long in Siam before his final victory over the Tay-sons. Northern civilians like Du were patronized but never generously admitted to the inner circles of the dynasty. And as late as 1836—sixteen years after Du's death, and at a time when Confucian civil service examinations rather than the "Bangkok honor roll" occupied the predominant place in Vietnamese political life—a bureaucrat serving in Du's home region in north-central Vietnam could still observe that "there is a great amount of differentiation between southerners and northerners: because southerners are lucky enough to be flatterers, everything that they say and do occupies the position of advantage, and northerners in their innermost thoughts consider themselves to be shamed." Du himself publicly epitomized, almost unnaturally, this psychology of shamed subservience. On the occasion of his death, in 1820, the official court "veritable records" characterized him as a "frightened man who, each time he presented himself at an imperial audience, was terrified and anxious and could not reply."

But the court chroniclers who produced this disdainful verdict had never made a greater error. Du was better able to reply than any other poet in Southeast Asia.

Out of his personal agonies, which were shared by a whole

generation of northern upper-class scholars who had had to come to terms with a cankered world of compromises, he described the complicated moral pilgrimage of Kieu. Kieu's story stood in effect as a parable of the questings and the sadnesses of his own political life. Merely to write such a poem might have been dangerous, though Du's talents as a "national poet" had won him the respect of the Nguyen rulers at the time of his death. A very thin shadow-line separated literature from sedition in late traditional Vietnam. The forty-seven moral injunctions of the Le emperors, first promulgated in 1663 and reissued in 1760, five years before Du was born, declared that only the "classics, histories, philosophy, belles-lettres and essays" could be printed and circulated among the Vietnamese population, that the "cutting of printing blocks and the engraving and printing" of "national tales" and of ballads and poems "which are associated with profligacy" were strictly forbidden. In the first year of Gia-long's reign, 1802, the uneducated soldier Nguyen Van Nhan, who candidly admitted that he had not begun to read Chinese texts himself until he was fifty years old, designed a program for local education, "deeply commended" by the emperor, which ordered Vietnamese children to read the Chinese Five Classics and threatened with swift punishment all villagers who had become "addicted to songs and ballads." In this culturally authoritarian environment, insecure rulers suspected that even the flutes and the gongs of the tiniest village theatrical groups might convey the most deadly iconoclasms.

To look for philosophical uniformities in *The Tale of Kieu* would of course be idle. Different philosophies mingle in the poem, and Confucian language mingles with Buddhist language. Yet the work is a moral tale in which the commonplace determinisms of Buddhist popular evangelism, while inevitably present, may well be sharply subdued. The Buddhist doctrine of "cause and effect"—the belief that there are inescapable relationships between present existences and past and future existences, and that crimes committed during past existences preordain miseries in the present—is prominent enough, but is it the central theme? Du does not make the slightest effort to portray anything but the current existence of Kieu. He divides her life into two parts, the time of misfortune and degradation which comes to an end when she throws herself into the "shoreless stream," the Ch'ien-t'ang River, and the time of restoration and happiness, after she is rescued, in which she is compensated for her sufferings. The Buddhist perspective that the full passions of love are "retribution," mechanically leading to more pain—"grief follows passion, that's the constant law," intones the prophetess Tam Hop—may not be of cardinal importance to Nguyen Du's extraordinary vision either. After all, he does not make Kieu regret her one lifelong love, but instead makes her fear that she has committed an offense against her lover, Kim Trong, by her forced ventures into decadence. Perhaps the real meaning of Nguyen Du (at least on one level) is that passion does not, by itself, bring punishment in the next world but must, to be moral, carry important redemptive self-denying obligations with it in this world. Morality is painful and difficult, and happiness is only a qualified, far from utopian reward at the end, not the constant comforting accompaniment of even the truly moral person. Despite its trappings of astrology and metempsychosis, the poem in this sense becomes a remarkable hymn to individual fortitude and individual moral responsibility.

What, however, would this signify in historical terms? Du's apparent emphasis upon properly conducted individual moral decision-making bringing moderate positive results in this world, rather than utopian salvation in the next, suggests a tougher, less mystical creed than those cherished by many other members of Vietnamese society in the early 1800's. Popular Buddhist movements among the peasantry—for example, the "Precious Mountain Miraculous Fragrance" *(Buu Son Ky Huong)* movement which evolved in Sa Dec province in the south in 1849—

rarely pretended that "hidden merits" could "tip the scale" in this world rather than in the next as a result of individual moral industry. As powerful Vietnamized offshoots of the Chinese White Lotus religion, they hoped instead for a dazzling apocalypse, for the time of the great "dragon flower" meeting when the messiah Buddha would descend to earth in a cloud of fragrant scents and ethereal fireworks and end all human tribulations. There appears to be, in short, an outlook in *The Tale of Kieu* that was by no means completely ordinary in early nineteenth-century Vietnam, an outlook that modern, more secularized Vietnamese intellectuals find hospitable and Vietnamese revolutionaries, faced with their own fatiguing and sometimes temporarily humiliating pilgrimages to a better future, find inspiring. The historian must take note of the surprisingly modern qualities in this work, as well as of its synoptic recitations of the vicissitudes of a bygone classical age.

Thanks to Huynh Sanh Thong's imaginative, painstaking artistry, a great literary synthesis of the Vietnamese experience has finally been imported into the English-speaking world. In this world, one historian is confident, the wandering soul of Nguyen Du will find more than a few admirers of a poignant if highly deceptive "tale of love recorded in old books."

Contents

Translator's Acknowledgments

This translation of Nguyen Du's poem is based on the best-known edition, entitled *Truyen Thuy Kieu*, by Bui Ky and Tran Trong Kim. It deviates from it in a few instances when alternative readings seem more valid.

In part or in whole, the first draft was exposed to the scrutiny of my students at Yale University: Clarence Abercrombie III, Joan Beckham (Mrs. John K. Whitmore), Theodora Bofman, David Bourquin, Thomas Fox, Richard S. D. Hawkins, Penelope Mendenhall (Mrs. John Pestle), and Carl Thayer. Whether sincere or well feigned, their response was such as to convince me that my project was not a completely hopeless attempt and to encourage me to persist.

Professor Rufus Hendon took time out from a demanding schedule to read one of the earlier drafts with care and make precious suggestions.

A distinguished scholar and translator of Chinese poetry, Professor James R. Hightower of Harvard University, gave me the benefit of his experience and wisdom.

Adrienne Suddard provided me with valuable comments on some sections of the manuscript.

Charles Benoit, Jr., a devoted student of *The Tale of Kieu*, lent me some books that are hard to find but essential to my work.

The Vietnam Studies Coordinating Group of the Association for Asian Studies has sponsored my research in Vietnamese literature and culture, and many of its members have proved themselves inspiring colleagues as well as generous friends, in particular Professors John K. Whitmore, Alexander B. Woodside, David G. Marr, and Truong Buu Lam.

In Anne Freedgood I have found an editor every author dreams of—someone who combines in equal measure the firmness of a critic and the good will of a friend.

Whatever merit this English version may claim owes much to all the persons listed above. If it still falls far short of the original and does scant justice to Vietnam's greatest poet and novelist, the reader must blame my deficiencies as a translator.

Hamden, Connecticut   Huynh Sanh Thong

Introduction

Annexed to the Chinese empire for some nine hundred years, Vietnam did not become an independent state until 939. Even then, the ruling elite clung to Chinese institutions as the best safeguards against reconquest. Classical Chinese remained the official language up to the second half of the nineteenth century, when the French took over.

But as national self-confidence grew, a movement arose to promote Vietnamese as a vehicle for creative expression. During the fourteenth century a demotic script called *chu nom* (Southern characters) first came into currency. It was a rather cumbersome system for representing the sounds of the vernacular with characters adapted from the Chinese, but it had an electrifying effect on literature, freeing the writer to explore and exploit the resources of his native culture.

The marriage of Chinese classical influences and Vietnamese folk traditions begot the most remarkable genre in Vietnamese literature, the long narrative poem known as *truyen nom*, or the "tale in the Southern script." Often based on Chinese works of prose fiction, the poems were written in a form accessible to the masses: *luc-bat,* or "six-eight," verse, the prevalent meter of folk poetry.

Reduced to a minimum, six-eight verse consists of a couplet of six syllables for the first line and eight syllables for the second, in contrast to the odd numbers of syllables (five or seven in each line) of most Chinese poetry.

Many Vietnamese folk poems are simply six-eight couplets, shorter than Japanese *haiku.* But any number of the couplets can be strung together into a continuous, unbroken whole without becoming monotonous. By using end rhymes and internal rhymes at the sixth syllable of an eight-syllable line, one can make each line rhyme with the next and at the same time introduce a different rhyme in every other line. Two more characteristics of six-eight verse should be noted: it is iambic, and the accented syllables follow a definite pattern of flat and sharp tones.

Since rhyme, meter and tonal regularity all make long stretches of six-eight verse easier to memorize and recite than most other forms of poetry, *luc-bat* is an ideal medium for oral transmission, perfectly adapted to the needs of a Vietnamese writer of long narrative poems. In traditional Vietnam, publication in book form was severely limited, not only because printing was primitive but also because of government curbs. Furthermore, only the educated minority could read books, since the "Southern script" presupposed an extensive knowledge of Chinese characters. The only way to reach the general public was to have professional or amateur bards learn the poems by heart and recite them.

The long narrative poem in six-eight verse, which developed during the seventeenth or eighteenth century, reached its culmination in *The Tale of Kieu,* by Nguyen Du (1766–1820). It must have been completed and circulated in manuscript for quite a few years before his death. Originally the author entitled it *Doan*

4

Truong Tan Thanh, which can be translated as New Cries from a Broken Heart. A friend, Pham Qui Thich (1760–1825), arranged a posthumous publication of the work, renaming it *Kim Van Kieu Tan Truyen*, or A New Version of the Tale of Kim, Van, and Kieu. But to millions of Vietnamese, it is known as *Truyen Kieu* (The Tale of Kieu), or simply as *Kieu*. A perfect example of the long narrative poem in six-eight verse, it has also stood unchallenged over the past hundred and fifty years as the supreme achievement of Vietnamese literature.

Both the original title and Pham Qui Thich's suggest that Nguyen Du did not make up the story himself but borrowed it from another source. It was, in fact, taken from a Chinese novel. Some early French writers seized upon this fact to dismiss the poem as a mere translation from the Chinese, conveniently forgetting that the most prized jewels of French literature, Corneille's and Racine's tragedies, La Fontaine's fables, can be traced to works by Greek or Roman authors.

Although the source of Nguyen Du's narrative poem remained an unsettled question for many decades, it is now tentatively agreed that he got the story from a Ming novel entitled *Chin Yün Ch'iao Chuan* (The Tale of Chin, Yün, and Ch'iao) by a writer who lived in the sixteenth century and called himself the Pure-Hearted Man of Parts (Ch'ing-hsin Ts'ai-jen). His real name was Hsü Wei, but he was also known as Wen-ch'ang, T'ien-ch'ih, and Ch'ing-t'eng. In 1554, during the Chia-ch'ing era, he was secretary to Governor Hu Tsung-hsien (Ho Ton Hien in Sino-Vietnamese) and took part in a campaign to suppress the revolt of the rebel Hsü Hai (Tu Hai in Sino-Vietnamese). Unable to vanquish him by force of arms, Hu bribed Hsü's concubine, a former courtesan named Wang Ts'ui-ch'iao (Vuong Thuy Kieu in Sino-Vietnamese); she persuaded the rebel to surrender, and he was killed. Forced to marry a "barbarian" (a tribal chief), Ts'ui-ch'iao drowned herself. Hsü Wei's first version of the story more or less faithfully records her life and death. Later on, however, after a period of insanity and many reverses of fortune, he became a devout Buddhist and appended a sequel to his novel in which Ts'ui-ch'iao is rescued and reunited with her family.

Nguyen Du's poem closely follows the events of this later version of Hsü Wei's novel. Yet while Hsü's novel is now ignored by all but a handful of Chinese literary specialists, Nguyen's poem has established itself as the great classic of Vietnam.

The poem's appeal to scholars is easy to understand. Nguyen Du pays loving attention to the fine points of a classical poet's craft. For example, when Kieu first sees the abandoned grave of Dam Tien, a courtesan, she contents herself with writing a *chüeh-chü* (cut-off lines) quatrain to commemorate the occasion. But after Dam Tien's ghost appears in answer to her prayer, Kieu is carried away—"a poet's feelings flowed and brooked no bounds"—and she writes a *ku-shih* (old style) poem, which is quite free, with no fixed number of lines and words in each line and with flexible rhyming schemes.

The *Kieu* poem is a treasure-trove of classical Chinese learning. A recent study made in Hanoi has found in it forty-six quotations from *The Book of Odes*, a Confucian anthology of verse; fifty references to other Confucian classics; fifty-seven translations or imitations of various Chinese poems; sixty-nine allusions to works of fiction; and twenty-one mentions of Buddhist or Taoist scriptures. Such vast erudition, if indiscriminately displayed in an imaginative work, runs the risk of boring or even offending. But in *Kieu* it is woven so gracefully into the fabric of the poem, it is so apposite to the purpose in each case, that it may elude the average reader while it surprises and delights the connoisseur. When Kieu is trapped in a second bawdy-house and complains of Heaven's cruelty toward women, she does so by a play on words: *Hong-quan* (Heaven) versus *hong-quan* ([those who wear] red skirts). Then, addressing *Hong-*

quan, she says, "You've spun me long enough—why don't you stop?" The metaphor takes the alert reader aback—suddenly he realizes that the expression *Hong-quan,* which is vaguely understood by most people as a way of indicating Heaven, God, the Creator, is being used here in its exact meaning of Great Potter's Wheel.

Nguyen Du's allusions to other poets and poems are also both pertinent and unobtrusive. Consider the line: "Birds thronged the branch, winds stirred the leaves." In context, it implies that Kieu attracts many customers to the brothel. While nobody can miss the point, a reader's enjoyment will be sharpened if he realizes that it is a neat paraphrase of two lines from a poem by a famous T'ang courtesan, Hsüeh T'ao, discussing her life: "The branch greets birds from south and north./ The leaves sway back and forth with winds." Similarly, Nguyen Du describes the rebel Tu Hai as follows: "He roved on streams and lakes, plying his oar,/ with sword and lute upon his shoulders slung." Anyone can picture Tu as a free spirit and a sensitive soul, but the informed reader will also recognize here the self-portrait of Huang Ch'ao, the T'ang scholar-rebel who captured Ch'ang-an in 880 and reigned briefly as emperor. Again, when Van urges her elder sister, Kieu, to wed Kim Trong after a fifteen-year separation, she says, "The boughs still have some three or seven plums!/ The peach tree's still quite fresh!" It is clear that she means that Kieu is not too old for matrimony, but the East Asian classicist will spot at once deft allusions to two songs of courtship and marriage in *The Book of Odes.*

Nguyen Du's artistry goes far beyond esoteric games, however. His poem illustrates the craft of fiction in its more universal aspects and deserves to be called a novel. His numerous, terse yet vivid, descriptions of nature, for example, never appear merely for their picturesque value but always perform a narrative or psychological function.

There is the cycle of seasons—"time flees on moon-hare's feet and sun-crow's wings"—as the plot unfolds. It all started on a beautiful third day of the third month: "Swift swallows and spring days were shuttling by—/ of ninety radiant ones three score had fled./ Young grasses spread a mat to the sky's rim,/ and blossoms put white speckles on pear boughs . . ." Summer begins: "As windy days and moonlit nights whirled round,/ red decreased, green increased, and spring was past . . ./ The cuckoos cried for summer 'neath the moon./ Above the wall, pomegranate trees displayed/ their fiery blooms . . ." And in the ominous autumn, leaves turn and things happen: "Now, in the yard, the *wu-t'ung* tree flashed gold./ Along the hedge, white buds of mums peeped out . . ." The seasonal circuit is also associated with the healing process of time, as when young Thuc gradually gets used to the (erroneous) idea that Kieu has perished in a fire: "Yet when the lotus dies, the asters bud—/ time softens pain, and winter turns to spring . . ."

When Kieu awakes to love and the possibility of sorrow after she has met Kim Trong and found Dam Tien's grave on the same day, the moon becomes a silent witness to the secrets of her soul torn between hopes and fears: "At the window the moon was peering in./ It splashed ripples of gold across the waves,/ projected dark tree shadows on the yard." When she slips out of her house at night to see Kim, she is observed: "a dappled moon was peeping through the leaves." At a crucial moment of their tryst, the lovers are not alone: ". . . while the moon was watching from the skies,/ with one voice both pronounced their sacred oath." Necessity compels her to break that oath, and as she follows Scholar Ma, who has bought her, she is painfully reminded of her betrayal: "A midnight path—a sky of hush and mist./ The moon, a witness to her vows, cried shame."

Not only the moon but nature as a whole joins in the story, providing a suitable background for the action, adumbrating forthcoming events or mirroring the state of mind of the chief protagonists. In Confucian society, for a nubile girl to obey her impulses and go to her lover's apartments was tantamount to a deadly sin, so Nguyen Du prepares the reader of his times for the shock. Seemingly innocent passages of description foreshadow Kieu's deed: "A camellia drooped east, toward the next house./ As dewdrops fell, the spring branch bent and bowed . . ./ Outside, an oriole began to chirp—/ a willow catkin dropped, to drift next door . . ." Again, the unaffected lyricism of folk poetry informs the depiction of a twilight scene viewed through Kieu's eyes as she, a prisoner in the brothel, wonders about her uncertain future: "She sadly watched the harbor in gray dusk—/ whose boat was that with fluttering sails, far off?/ She sadly watched the river flow to sea—/ those flowers adrift and lost, where would they end?/ She sadly watched the sweep of wilted grass,/ the pale-blue haze where mingled earth and sky./ She sadly watched the wind play with the waves/ that roared and rolled about, beneath her seat."

Despite the strict economy of a poem in which less than thirty-five hundred lines encompass a host of incidents, Nguyen Du qualifies as a novelist in the modern sense by the range of techniques he brings to bear on character delineation. With precise strokes, he conjures up a gallery of portraits that live in both their physical presence and their psychological identity. Here is Kim Trong, "a scion of the noblest stock" endowed with the expected attributes of a member of the Confucian aristocracy yet memorable in himself:

> They saw a youthful scholar come their way
> astride a colt he rode with slackened rein.
> He carried half a bagful of love poems,
> and page-boys tended him, tagging behind.
> His frisky horse had a coat white as snow.
> His gown commingled tints of grass and sky . . .
> In his embroidered shoes he trod the grass,
> a figure shining like ruby and jade . . .

From a clan blessed with talent and with wealth,
nature and nurture both had formed his mind.
Looks and manners set him above the crowd.
At home he led the gracious life of books,
and in the world he gave with open hand . . .

Although Nguyen Du uses the clichés that embody Chinese canons of feminine beauty, he succeeds in contrasting the two Vuong sisters—"lissome of body, pure of soul, each girl/ was her own self and perfect in her way." Designed for a tranquil, contented life, the younger sister evinces a somewhat dull, placid sort of comeliness: "In dignity, Van was beyond compare—/ her face a moon, her eyebrows two full curves;/ her smile a flower, her voice the sound of jade;/ her hair the sheen of clouds, her skin like snow." We do not count on her to feel deeply about anything, and when she scolds Kieu for crying over Dam Tien's grave her words ring true: "Sister, you truly make me laugh, . . ./ wasting your tears on one long dead and gone!" On the other hand, Kieu's melancholy charm and artistic temperament indicate a predisposition to sorrow: "Her eyes were autumn streams, her brows spring hills./ The flowers and willows envied her fresh hue./ A glance or two from her, and cities rocked!/ Supreme in loveliness, she had few peers/ in skills and arts. By Heaven graced with wit,/ she learned to rhyme and paint, and she could sing./ In music she had mastered all five tones/ and played the lute far better than Ai Chang./ She had composed a tune called 'Cruel Fate'/ to mourn all women in soul-rending strains . . ."

But it is in the portrayal of villains that Nguyen Du's brush, unhampered by the dead weight of stereotypes, is most striking. Here is Ma, scholar turned pimp: "Past forty, he had left his youth behind,/ but still he wore smart clothes and a smooth face . . ./ Ma long had patronized the haunts of lust./ Much whoring and some strokes of blackest luck/ had ruined him: the scholar settled down/ in harlotdom to work for bed and board." Ma comes most palpably to life when he is allowed to speak in his own behalf. In this soliloquy, he is debating whether he should exercise his marital rights or deliver Kieu intact to his wife, Dame Tu, who runs a brothel:

"The maid lies in my power! . . .
He waves the flag who holds it in his hand!
The more I view her charms, the more I rave!
Celestial hue! Unearthly scent! Her price
is far above all gold and no mistake!
When she gets there, to pluck the maiden bud
princes and gentlefolk will push and shove.
She'll bring at least three hundred or about
what I have paid for her. And after that,
all she will earn is profit, net and clear.
But when a tidbit dangles at your mouth,
should you protect the money you invest
or should you eat what Heaven has served up?
A peach divine within a mortal's grasp!
Well, let me bend the branch and pick the fruit
and gobble it to make my life complete!
How many flower collectors in the world
can really tell one rose from the next rose?
Juice from pomegranate skin and cockscomb blood,
in proper mixture, lend the pristine look—
in the half-light, a yokel will be fooled!
Though less than new, no less money she'll fetch.
If the old girl finds out and makes a scene,
I'll bear it like a man, upon my knees!
In any case, it's a long journey home—
if I don't go near her, I'll look suspect."

From the monologue we can surmise that the academic pimp has met more than his match in the "old girl"—"whose once rich charms were taxed by creeping age." We catch a glimpse of her outward appearance: "She struck one at first glance with her pale skin—/ but what did she gorge on to gain such bulk?"

The bawd's vulgarity, however, can be conveyed in full only in her own words, which she pours out when she learns that Ma has tampered with Kieu:

> Her devils, fiends, and demons all broke loose.
> "It's plain what happened, what they did!" she shrieked.
> "You, strumpet, stole my man for your own use!
> I sent him off for girls to bring back here
> and train as hostesses—that's how we eat!
> But the false-hearted knave, the beastly swine
> had his damn itch and messed around with you!
> Now that the cloth has lost its glaze and starch,
> there goes to hell the money I put up!
> You little slut, they sold you to me here,
> and in my house you go by my house rules.
> When that old lecher stooped to his foul tricks,
> why did you fail to slap him in the face?
> Why did you just lie there and take it all?
> Young as you were, did you already rut?
> I must teach you how I lay down the law!"

Miss Hoan is in a class by herself as a villain. The daughter of a Chief Minister, she is married to young Thuc, who prefers the charms of a prostitute. Ferocious in her jealousy and wounded pride, she still commands our admiration by her self-control and ability to present a brave front to the world in spite of her husband's escapade:

> His garden boasted now a new-blown rose—
> so she had heard from every mouth but his.
> The fire of wrath kept smoldering in her breast
> against the knave whose fickle heart had roamed:
> "If only he had told me the whole truth,
> I might have favored her with my good grace.
> It would have been uncouth to lose my calm
> and gain the stigma of a jealous shrew.
> But he thought fit to play his boyish prank
> and hide his open secret, who knows why!
> He must have fancied distance made it safe

to keep things back from me—well, we shall see!
I entertain no worry on this head.
The ant's inside the cup—where could it crawl?
I shall make them abhor each other's sight!
Her I shall crush and trample underfoot!
In his false face I shall rub sweet revenge!
The villain thinks he'll scuttle this old boat,
but he shall know of what mettle I'm made!"

This is a preview of what is lying in store for Thuc and Kieu:

She locked her anger up inside her heart
and let the breezy tales blow past her ears.
One day, two louts came bringing a report
and hoped to earn fair wages for their pains.
The lady in high dudgeon thundered forth:
"I loathe those malaperts who'd spin a yarn!
My husband's not a common, vulgar churl!
Mouths with less truth than froth have spat this lie!"
She bade her lackeys give them their deserts,
slapping their mouths and knocking out their teeth.
An awe-struck hush now settled on her house—
nobody risked another single peep.
In her red chamber, day and night, she'd spend
her vacant hours—composed, she'd talk and laugh
as though nothing at all were out of joint.

She will give a hellish time to her rival—yet it is part of
Nguyen Du's humane touch to make us feel much sympathy for
the "lioness." She is defending the integrity of her home. As she
puts her case before Kieu at the trial, "I'm but a woman with
a woman's faults!/ And jealousy is human, after all! . . ./ In my
own heart I felt esteem for you,/ but what woman would gladly
share her man?" When Kieu forgives her and lets her go, mercy
is not unfounded on justice.

When a highborn lady eschews rhetoric and speaks the plain
language of passion, it is realism—an important facet of Nguyen
Du's artistry which endears him to a large public. Linked to such
fidelity to life is his sense of comedy, a rare attribute in a classical

poet. It was deemed far beneath the dignity of a Confucian gentleman to smile, let alone laugh. With few exceptions, classical Vietnamese literature presents an air of grim seriousness at best and dismal gloom at worst, a lack of gaiety that fails to reflect the temperament of the average, un-Confucianized Vietnamese who can joke under the most solemn or trying circumstances; colloquial speech is rich in words and phrases for mirth and derision.

Nguyen Du imparts an ironic twist to a learned cliché like "fish grass and tench" (*ch'un hsü* in Chinese). Automatically used to evoke homesickness, it alludes to the Chinese scholar Chang Han who resigned from office and went home on an autumn day because he missed the taste of those two common dishes of his native countryside. In *The Tale of Kieu*, it is used to suggest that young Thuc is getting bored with domestic felicity and his wife and wants to rush back to his true love, Kieu—"a homely diet of fish grass and tench/ soon palled his appetite." This kind of wit, however, is over the head of a reader unfamiliar with the allusion. Sometimes Nguyen Du lets a ludicrous situation speak for itself:

Between, festooned with wreaths of incense smoke,
there hung on high the image of a god—
the White-Browed God. For in all Green Pavilions
(or bawdyhouses) custom so prescribed—
he was worshiped as patron saint by whores
and offered flowers and incense night and day.
When luck forsook a girl and trade was slow,
in front of him she'd doff her shirt and skirt.
Stripped to the skin, she would intone a prayer
and burn a votive bunch of incense sticks;
then on the altar she would place fresh flowers;
the faded ones she'd take to line her bed—
and presto, bees would swarm from miles around!

More often, for comic relief, he draws on the inexhaustible supply of folk sayings, which he chooses with an uncanny flair. How else can one poke fun at the marriage of an aging prostitute and an aging debauchee but in these words: "Upon one common ground two met and merged—/ she swapped her sawdust for his bitter melon . . ."? The proverbial phrase "sawdust and bitter melon" *(mat cua muop dang)* comes from a folk tale: a hawker who foisted sawdust *(mat cua)* as rice bran on customers met another who passed bitter melons *(muop dang)* off for cucumbers—the two traded their goods, swindling each other.

Yet, despite the squalor and sordidness in the story, *The Tale of Kieu* is basically a romance—another reason for its enduring popularity. Love is the subject of many Vietnamese tales in verse, but all its richness and diversity have never been as well portrayed as by Nguyen Du. "Unbidden, love will come to those it picks"—and for Kieu it picks three men: Kim Trong, Thuc Ky Tam, and Tu Hai. "When two kindred souls meet, one single tie/ will bind them both in one unslipping knot"—still, each tie has its own texture and resiliency.

With Kim, it was love at first sight: "what their hearts felt, their eyes still dared not say." Nguyen Du knows how to express the psychic turmoil that accompanies an adolescent's discovery of the other sex: "How strange the race of lovers! Try as one will,/ one can't unsnarl their hearts' entangled threads." Seldom has the erratic comportment of a boy in the throes of love been rendered with such acute yet affectionate perception, as if Nguyen Du were reminiscing about his own youth and mocking himself:

> Back in his room, surrounded by his books,
> Kim could not shut Kieu's image from his mind.
> He drained the cup of gloom—it filled anew;
> one day away from her: three autumns long.
> Now silken curtains veiled her like a cloud—
> he moved in the world's dust but lived in dreams.

As the moon waned and the lamp sputtered low,
his face yearned for her face, his heart for hers.
The study-room grew still and cold as ice—
brushes lay dry, lute strings hung loose on frets.
A rustling breeze played music on the blinds.
He vainly kindled incense and drank tea,
craving her scent and missing love's sweet taste.
Unless the heavens destined her for him,
why had the temptress come and teased his eyes?
Racked with desire, he pictured place and girl:
he rushed back to the scene where they had met.
He could still view the meadow, lush and green,
and the unmuddied stream—but nothing more.
The breeze at twilight stirred a mood of woe—
the sedges shook their heads in seeming taunts.
Fancy supplies all that the mind forgets—
in search of Kieu, he dashed toward the Blue Bridge . . .

According to Confucian ethics it was unspeakable for a well-bred girl to meet a boy in secret in his room—yet Nguyen Du convinces us of the purity of Kieu's motives and gives us a romantic heroine's eloquent case for premarital continence:

"Of love don't make a game!" she chided him.
"Please stay away from me and let me speak.
On the peach tree I am too plain a bud
to venture fending off the Bluebird's quest.
But I'm your promised wife—and for her man
a bride must keep her soul and body pure.
If like the maids in those mulberry-groves
on the P'u River banks I misbehaved,
would you still sue for such a wench's hand?
If we reached out and seized the moment's thrill,
we'd damage in one day a lifelong trust.
Of all the lovers sung by ancient bards,
which other pair could equal Ts'ui and Chang?
And yet excess destroyed their plighted troth:
she humored all his whims and killed their love.
As wing to wing and limb to limb they lay,

contempt already lurked inside their hearts.
In time love's fire went out. They broke the vows
that in the Western Chamber both had sworn—
their love, unblessed with wedlock, died in shame.
If I don't cast the shuttle to resist
and guilt should haunt our lives, who should be blamed?
Why force your wish on a shy flower so soon?
Before I die, you'll one day get your due!"

Kim is never to get his due, however. At the end of the story, he and Kieu are reunited and joined in wedlock, but the union remains unconsummated. He reluctantly complies with her scruples: "Must lovers share one pillow and one mat/ to live in concord like zither and harp? . . ./ Their wishes all came true as fate so willed,/ and of two lovers marriage made two friends."

But it would be a mistake to conclude from this that Nguyen Du was a prude. He is one of the very few classical East Asian poets to celebrate physical love frankly but within the bounds of good taste. He cannot be accused of pandering to any prurient interest—a mildly pornographic passage in the original Chinese novel is reduced in his poem to this professional lecture by the bawd:

"The trade of love does take much toil and care,
and we who ply the trade must know its tricks! . . .
If girls were all alike, . . .
why would the men come here and spend their gold?
There are more things to love than meet the eye,
and ways to cope with men by day or dark.
My daughter, here they are—know them by rote.
Learn seven steps to snare and capture men.
Learn all eight ways to pleasure them in bed.
Play love with them till you've played them all out—
till heads will swim, till hearts of stone will spin!
Now flirt with eyes, now feign anger with brows.
Now sing the moon, now disport among flowers.

There you have it, this house's stock in trade!
Possess it all—you'll have mastered your art!"

The love between Kieu and the weak-willed Thuc eventually matures into a deep attachment, but sexual attraction is its main ingredient, and Nguyen Du takes care to stress the point. Here is homage paid to Kieu's beauty: "A woman's charms, O wondrous tidal waves—/ they sweep away a fortress like a toy! . . ./ Such pure-white ivory, such unblemished jade—/ her body stood as Heaven's masterwork!" And sexual intercourse is described in a restrained but intense manner:

Behind the tasseled drapes he faced the flower;
his fancy feasted on her every charm:
on its young stem the camellia in bloom
would glow still brighter with each fresh spring shower!
Man and girl, girl and man—one fevered flesh:
on a spring night, how could they quell their blood?

We are made to feel the poignancy of the lovers' grief when they have to part: "She walked back home to face the night alone,/ and by himself he fared the distant way./ Who split their moon? Half stayed upon her pillow,/ half followed him along his journey's road."

In most ways the opposite of Thuc, Tu Hai is the strong man whom Kieu can look up to and lean on. When "eyes met eyes and heart encountered heart," she is shrewd enough to sense his potential greatness. He is both flattered by and grateful for her keen insight:

"My soul has found its mate! . . .
I do not play at love like giddy fools.
I've heard them rave about your charms and moan
that none of them earned grace in your clear eyes.
But then how often do you see a man
and not a fish in bowl or bird in cage? . . .
How many friends . . .
have understood my soul? But your sharp eyes

have seen the hero hidden in the dust!
You spoke one word that proved you've read my thoughts.
If I should conquer myriad pecks of grain
and win a thousand chariots by main force,
I shall still keep you always at my side!"

Tu feels for Kieu a tender, protective, indulgent kind of love; he wants to right the wrongs she has suffered, see to her comfort and well-being, grant her every wish and desire. In the end, he meets his doom because he "let a woman warp a hero's will." She rightly takes full blame for his death:

"He trusted me and did what I advised—
that fighter who had never lost a fight
agreed to lay down arms and serve at court!
He hoped to gain the world for him and me—
alas, he came to nothing in a trice!"

In addition to its romance, Nguyen Du's poem shares other features with works of fiction that have a mass appeal. It is a melodrama that pulsates with violent incidents, including war:

Vapors of slaughter rose and blurred the air,
as rivers teemed with men who fought like sharks
and roads with killers swathed in coats of mail . . .
The murk of death that none on earth could breathe
billowed in angry fumes to choke the skies . . .

It is a story that caters to folk beliefs in supernatural phenomena: the brooding presence of Dam Tien's ghost, fortune-telling, witchcraft, Tu Hai's deification in death. The Vietnamese people have given *The Tale of Kieu* a final accolade in this respect: they have consulted it for divination purposes, to which it lends itself very well because, within its scope, it covers most life circumstances, from the highest to the lowest, the happiest to the saddest.

But literary merit alone cannot explain the spell Nguyen Du's poem has cast over the Vietnamese, peasants and scholars alike.

They all have found in it some common denominator, some truth about their world that touches a chord in their collective psyche.

A major clue, perhaps, is a word that keeps recurring throughout the poem: *oan*. The nearest equivalent in English is a past participle: "wronged." A story purporting to recount events that took place in Ming China manages to project one stark, readily recognizable image about Vietnam—the picture of a society of victims, of people punished for crimes and sins they did not commit.

Over the past two thousand years, despotic government has been the norm in Vietnam. Direct Chinese rule lasted for almost a millennium until 939. To survive constant Chinese pressure, independent Vietnamese monarchs had to adopt Chinese political institutions and impose on a tropical Southeast Asian environment all the austerity of Confucian ideology, all the sternness of a state apparatus more compatible with the bleaker landscape of China.

In theory, the king acted as the "lamp of Heaven" *(den Troi)*, shining justice on all, but in practice he never would or could get close enough to the people to know their grievances: "Now only Heaven could redress this wrong—/ alas, just Heaven ruled so far away! . . ./ For justice can we cry, we flies and ants?" To administer justice throughout the realm, the king had to depend on local scholar-officials who, often underpaid in a subsistence economy, were tacitly encouraged to live off their charges. Corruption was built into the system; in dealing with officials, the people must "reckon up how much it all would cost/ to bribe and pave this way or clear that path."

There were high-principled mandarins, of course, but even they tended to maintain a decorous aloofness from the populace, lest familiarity should breed contempt and undermine authority —"Play with a dog, and it will lick your face" *(choi voi cho, cho liem mat)*, says the proverb. Actually the mandarins themselves were underlings—clerks and scribes, bailiffs and runners. In a position to bully and to squeeze, they were the most feared and hated members of the bureaucracy: "for money they would maim and murder, too." Rare were the officeholders who did not abuse their borrowed power: "there was old Chung, a scribe,/ who felt compassion that belied his trade." Nguyen Du shows us how "the myrmidons put in a good day's work" as they storm Kieu's house:

Armed to the teeth with knives and wooden staves,
they madly ran around, more beasts than men.
They clapped a cangue on father and on son,
and with a single rope they trussed both up.
Then, like bluebottles buzzing through the place,
they broke workbaskets and handlooms to bits;
they grabbed at goods and chattels, odds and ends,
picking all corners clean to fill their sacks . . .
A fear-struck household was turned upside down.
The air was rent with cries of innocence
and shrill protests against iniquity.
All day, the victims groveled and crouched low,
pleading to stone-deaf ears. Father and son
were beaten black-and-blue, then to a beam
their feet were tied—they dangled there, heads down.
The piteous sight would have softened a rock—
their features twisted in dire pain and fear.

What crime were the Vuong father and son guilty of to call down such punishment? A laconic line refers to unspecified charges brought by "some knave who sold raw silk." The failure to give any definite information might be regarded as a lapse in narrative skill, but it points up the arbitrary nature of the arrest: on the flimsiest of grounds, lives could be wrecked at the whim of those in power.

For the three hundred taels of silver needed to ransom her father, Kieu sells herself as a "concubine" to Scholar Ma, the pimp, and is unwittingly swept into a life of turpitude. Like

Kieu, many people in an unjust society have been struck by "disasters that come flying on the wind" *(va gio tai bay)*, by inexplicable catastrophes, and they have empathized with her lot, feeling no reluctance to identify with a harlot. If Confucian moralists condemn women who "traffic in powder and perfume" *(buon phan ban huong)*, the people take a kinder view of those who must "sell their rumps to feed their mouths" *(ban tron nuoi mieng)*. Prostitution is a temporary necessity from which a woman will escape at the first chance. According to a folk saying, "A whore works in nine places and saves one place where to get a husband" *(lam di chin phuong, de mot phuong lay chong)*. The ethical authority of marriage and the family is such that a man may "make a whore his wife, not his wife a whore" *(lay di lam vo, khong ai lay vo lam di)*. Kieu the prostitute conforms to that ingrained prejudice in favor of marriage and the family: she runs away with the cad So Khanh in the mistaken hope that he will make an honest woman of her; she asks for a concubine's modest niche in Thuc's home ("Should she, displeased, object and raise a storm,/ tell her I know my place and honor hers"); she attains transient respectability as the consort of the rebel Tu Hai during his five-year period of victories; in the end, she is reunited with Kim Trong, who generously accepts her as a platonic bride; and she expresses her gratitude in these terms: "If my body is ever cleansed of stains,/ I'll bless a gentleman, a noble soul! . . ./ A roof, a refuge you have offered me—/ my honor lives again as of tonight!"

More sinned against than sinning, Kieu as a folk symbol stands for the victim's struggle to survive by drawing comfort and sustenance from a mixture of the popular belief in Heaven's will and the Buddhist concept of fate: "All things are fixed by Heaven, first and last./ Heaven appoints each creature to a place . . ./ A Karma each of us has to live out:/ let's stop decrying Heaven's quirks and whims."

It is easy to see how the masses find catharsis and solace in

Kieu, but members of the Vietnamese elite have looked upon her as their alter ego as well. Indeed, it can even be claimed that in the plaintive voice of a girl sold into prostitution and slavery, Nguyen Du himself airs personal discontents with his official career. At the start and finish of his tale he seems to drop hints as to his real purpose: "A hundred years—in this life span on earth,/ how apt to clash, talent and destiny! . . ./ In talent take no overweening pride—/ great talent and misfortune make a pair." In classical literature, when talent is deplored as the target of fate, it belongs to a man rather than to a woman: "talent for men, beauty for women" *(trai tai, gai sac),* as the adage goes.

The poem also contains a lively debate on women's chastity and fidelity. Toward the end of the story, when Kim urges Kieu to abide by her old vow and marry him in spite of all that has happened to her, she answers:

"A happy home where love will reign, . . .
who does not dream of it? But I believe
a bride must bring her man the purity
of an unopened flower, the perfect shape
of a full moon. Priceless is chastity.
How could I put my dowry on display
under the nuptial torch, before your eyes? . . .
I can't think of myself and fail to blush—
how dare I soil with the world's dust and dirt
the homespun costume of a virtuous wife? . . ."

But Kim will not yield to her line of reasoning and retorts:

"Such artful dodges words invent! . . .
But there's more than one side, more than one truth.
Among those duties falling to her lot,
a woman's chastity means many things,
for there are times of ease and times of stress.
In crisis must all the commands apply?
You sold yourself and proved a daughter's love,
and in this way preserved your chastity.
What dust or dirt could ever sully you? . . ."

Such verbal give-and-take is reminiscent of an animal tale in verse, *Trinh Thu* (The Constant Mouse), written by a Vietnamese scholar presumably in the nineteenth century. It is about a she-mouse who, in the absence of her husband, resists the advances of a rat and refutes all his arguments against chastity and fidelity. If classical writers seem obsessed with the notion that women should remain immaculate in thought and deed, a student of East Asian literatures realizes that, more often than not, the issue serves as an allegory for a crucial problem in feudal times: political allegiance. For example, the T'ang poet Chang Chi (765-830) responded to overtures from the rebel Li Shih-tao with a poem entitled "Song of a Chaste Wife" *(Chieh fu yin):*

> My lord, you knew I had a husband—
> yet you sent me two shiny pearls.
> Affected by your loving thought,
> I sewed them to my red gauze blouse.
> My home stands tall near the Imperial Park.
> My man bears arms and guards the Radiant Hall.
> I know your pure heart glows like sun and moon—
> but to my man I'm pledged for life or death.
> I give you back your pearls with my two tears.
> Oh why had you and I not met before?

What we know of Nguyen Du's life seems to confirm the suspicion that he visualized himself as a political Kieu, a man forced to betray his loyalties and convictions in order to shield his family from harm. Although he belonged to a prominent Northern clan whose members had served the Le, the Trinh, and the Tay-son, he became a courtier in Hué, serving the Southern upstarts—the Nguyen. In 1802, with the help of French missionaries and mercenaries, Nguyen Anh emerged as the victor in a long civil war, and assuming the title of Gia-long, unified Vietnam. In all likelihood, the poet rallied to the winning side less out of enthusiasm than fear that his clan, badly compromised with Nguyen Anh's erstwhile enemies, might be persecuted. The theme of filial piety runs like a litany through his poem. Though he was highly regarded by both Gia-long and Minh-mang, Nguyen Du's proud nature never adjusted to the stifling atmosphere of Hué, where a young, insecure dynasty ruthlessly crushed any sign of insubordination. It is reported that while he acted humble at court, he maintained a glum reserve and was afflicted with an incurable melancholia until his death. His secret sentiments and dreams apparently flowed into the creation of the most astonishing character in his poem: Tu Hai.

In the original Chinese novel, Hsü Hai is little more than a pirate chief or a warlord. Nguyen Du's rebel, on the contrary, rises to epic heights—a hero *sans peur et sans reproche*, admired even by Ho Ton Hien who sets out to destroy him:

A tiger's beard, a jaw like swallow's beak,
brows thick as silkworms—tough and fierce, his looks.
His shoulders broad, he stood full ten spans tall.
A towering hero on the battlefield,
he overwhelmed his foes with club or fist
and was adept in all the arts of war.
In all the world he knew no law but his . . .
    From victory to victory Tu swept—
a slit bamboo will split all by itself,
and one slipped tile will topple the whole roof.
His fame like thunder rumbled far and wide.
In his own territory, he held court
and named his ministers for war and peace.
His fiefdom cleft the empire in two halves.
Time after time he stormed across the land
and trampled down five strongholds in the South.
He fought and honed his sword on wind and dust,
turning his back on all who were content
to serve as racks for coats and bags for rice.
At will he ruled the empire's borderland—

there he proclaimed himself a prince, a king.
Under his flag none dared dispute his sway.
For five years, by the sea, he reigned sole lord.

When he is asked to trade his independence for a high post at court, Tu Hai's thoughts no doubt reflect Nguyen Du's own loathing for a courtier's role:

"My own two hands have built this realm of mine.
I roam the streams and seas just as I wish.
If I submit, surrender all my power,
and show my shamed, confounded face at court,
what will become of me among them all?
Why let them swaddle me in robes and skirts?
Why play a duke only to cringe and fawn?
Better indeed to rule my own domain!
What can they really do against my might?
At pleasure I storm heaven and stir earth!
I come and go bowing my head to none!"

But listening to Kieu's advice, Tu Hai surrenders and falls into an ambush. Great in life, he looms larger yet in death:

The fiercest tiger, taken unawares,
will be entrapped and meet an abject end!
Facing his doom, Tu fought his one last fight
and showed them all a soldier's dauntless heart.
When his brave soul left him to join the gods,
he still stood on his feet amidst his foes,
remaining firm as rock and hard as bronze—
who in the world could shake or move his corpse?

In Confucian society, rebellion is *the* cardinal sin—yet here is a courtier singing a rebel's life and death in rapturous accents. If Nguyen Du jettisoned the Chinese model, he did not create Tu Hai wholly out of his unaided imagination. In the early part of the nineteenth century, Vietnam still reverberated to the echoes of a real-life epic—the meteoric career of Nguyen Hue. Flaunting his "cotton shirt and red flag" *(ao vai co dao),* he led

26

the Tay-son revolt to one of the greatest triumphs in the history of peasant uprisings. He defeated the Trinh lords in the North and the Nguyen lords in the South, and in 1789 he launched a New Year's offensive to rout the two hundred thousand invading troops of the Chinese emperor Ch'ien-lung: "in wit and valor second to no man,/ he shook and awed the heavens with his might." His reign as Emperor Quang-trung was ephemeral—after his death in 1792, at the age of forty, the Tay-son dynasty soon fell apart.

Along with the heroine, the portrait of Tu Hai, inspired by a genuine folk hero, firmly fixes *The Tale of Kieu* in the Vietnamese people's affections. As figures that carry the hopes and dreams of the downtrodden and the disinherited, prostitute and rebel complement each other. If she personifies passive resistance to injustice and oppression, he embodies a man's ability to break through the evil system and take the law into his own hands, redressing wrongs and rewarding virtues; the trial scene, where he lets her pay foes and friends their due wages, is a favorite with most Vietnamese.

But the significance of Nguyen Du's poem transcends both private anguish and popular identification. By an accident of history, the autobiography of a divided soul has come to epitomize a moral crisis that confronts all Vietnamese—scholars and intellectuals, in particular. From 1862 on, political allegiance became the paramount question they all had to answer in some way as the Hué court was forced to cede the three eastern provinces in the South to France. Phan Thanh Gian committed suicide after the further loss, in 1867, of the three western provinces entrusted to his care. The blind poet Nguyen Dinh Chieu totally ignored the enemy, turning down offers of financial aid, refusing to wash with French-made soap or walk on French-built roads. Other scholars like Ton-that Thuyet and Phan Dinh Phung organized resistance groups, which disintegrated under superior fire power. Less hardy spirits chose the

27

safest course: they collaborated with the French occupation forces.

When scholars and intellectuals accept a foreign master and do his bidding for the sake of wealth and rank, their behavior is properly called prostitution. In his controversy with Phan Van Tri after 1862, the collaborationist Ton Tho Tuong wrote a poem apologizing for his pro-French conduct and comparing Kieu's plight and his own—"when evil strikes, one bows to circumstance." Like Nguyen Du, Ton was never reconciled to what he did; toward the end of his life, in another poem, he likened himself to an old whore who had become a Buddhist nun and fasted for penitence.

During the 1920s and '30s, a passionate political debate revolved around *The Tale of Kieu.* The Director of Political Affairs for French Indochina, Louis Marty, appointed a brilliant scholar, Pham Quynh, to preside over a cultural movement that would advance French interests. Its chief organ, the review *Nam Phong,* undertook a detailed study of *The Tale of Kieu* in order to prove that there was nothing to fear in French influence because, in Pham's often-quoted words, "as long as *The Tale of Kieu* lasts, our language will last; as long as our language lasts, our country will last." Deliberately glossing over the ambiguities in Kieu's character, Pham canonized her and proclaimed *The Tale of Kieu* a "pure" masterpiece, subtly suggesting similar "pure" literary pursuits as a glorious (and profitable) alternative to politics or revolution.

Vietnamese intellectuals who opposed French rule, notably Ngo Duc Ke and Huynh Thuc Khang, recognized what Pham was doing and sought to denounce him. Under the watchful eyes of the French secret police, they could do this only obliquely. They attacked *The Tale of Kieu* as poisonous trash and its heroine as a depraved sinner. Because Pham had preempted one extreme of the critical spectrum, they went to the other to dramatize their opposition to the man they considered the most dangerous henchman of French colonialism. If *The Tale of Kieu* was everything to a traitor, then it was nothing to patriots. Yet there is no proof that the poem has ever dampened political zeal or cooled revolutionary ardor. The young Communist terrorist Ly Tu Trong read it in his cell just before he was led unrepentant to the guillotine. Ho Chi Minh himself knew many *Kieu* lines by heart and incorporated them into his own verse, although he never undertook a Marxist interpretation of the poem.

In the last third of the twentieth century, Nguyen Du's masterpiece is again in the minds of all thoughtful Vietnamese. The American crusade for a world untainted by Communism has torn asunder the warp and woof of society in South Vietnam and produced prostitution, both sexual and otherwise, on an unprecedented scale. Until the Vietnamese people can shape their own destiny free from the stranglehold of a foreign superpower, countless Vietnamese women and men will see themselves as Kieu—victims of a perverse fate.

The Tale of Kieu

I

A hundred years—in this life span on earth,
how apt to clash, talent and destiny!
Men's fortunes change even as nature shifts—
the sea now rolls where mulberry fields grew.[1]
One watches things that make one sick at heart.
This is the law: no gain without a loss,
and Heaven hurts fair women for sheer spite.

  By lamplight turn these scented leaves and read
a tale of love recorded in old books.
Once, when Chia-ch'ing[2] sat on the throne of Ming,
all lived in peace—both Capitals[3] were safe.
  In the Vuong clan there was an alderman
of modest wealth and station in the world.
He had a last-born son, Vuong Quan—his hope
to carry on a line of learnèd folk.
Two girls, both beautiful, had come before:

Thuy Kieu the elder, the younger Thuy Van.
Lissome of body, pure of soul, each girl
was her own self and perfect in her way.

In dignity, Van was beyond compare—
her face a moon, her eyebrows two full curves;
her smile a flower, her voice the sound of jade;
her hair the sheen of clouds, her skin like snow.
Yet Kieu possessed a keener, deeper charm—
she excelled Van in talent and in looks.
Her eyes were autumn streams, her brows spring hills.
The flowers and willows envied her fresh hue.
A glance or two from her, and cities rocked![4]
Supreme in loveliness, she had few peers
in skills and arts. By Heaven graced with wit,
she learned to rhyme and paint, and she could sing.
In music she had mastered all five tones[5]
and played the lute[6] far better than Ai Chang.[7]
She had composed a tune called 'Cruel Fate'
to mourn all women in soul-rending strains.

No girl of gentle birth could rival Kieu.
In the spring flush of youth she neared that time
when maidens pinned their hair[8] in solemn rites.
Still sheltered, she was kept behind drawn drapes.
Outside the Eastern wall,[9] her suitors swarmed
like bees and butterflies and left unseen.

Swift swallows and spring days were shuttling by—
of ninety radiant ones three score had fled.
Young grasses spread a mat to the sky's rim,
and blossoms put white speckles on pear boughs.
Now came the Feast of Light[10] in the third month,
with graveyard rites and outings on the green.
As merry pilgrims flocked from far and near,
Quan and his sisters went for a spring stroll.

Fine men and comely women on parade!
A crush of clothes! A rush of wheels and steeds!
Over the huddled graves they strewed and burned
sham gold and paper coins, and ashes flew. . .
    Then when the sun was dipping in the west,
the young folk hand in hand started for home.
In leisured steps they walked along a brook,
admiring here and there a pretty view.
The streamlet ran and wound its bubbly course
beneath a little bridge that spanned the banks.
Beside the road loomed up a mound of earth
with shriveled weeds, half yellow and half green.
    Kieu, puzzled, asked: "Now is the Feast of Light—
why is no incense burning for this grave?"
Vuong Quan told her this tale from first to last:
"Dam Tien, the singer, was a harlot, too.
Renowned for looks and gifts, she had her day.
A pack of lovers jostled at her door.
Alas, a rose is fragile. In mid-spring,
the rose stem broke—the fragrant bloom was dead.
From a far land a stranger came one day
to woo and win this girl of high repute.
But when the lover's boat sailed into port,
the pin had snapped in two, the pitcher sunk![11]
Her chamber, empty now, was cold and still.
Wheel tracks were vanishing beneath the moss.
He wept, full of a grief no words could tell:
'How harsh the fate that has kept us apart!
Since in this life we are not meant to meet,
let me pledge you my troth for our next life.'
He then procured a coffin and a hearse,
and in this shallow grave laid her to rest—
among the weeds and flowers. For many moons,
no kin nor friend has come to claim this tomb,

and no one has stopped here to pay respects."
    A well of pity lay within Kieu's heart—
as soon as she had heard, her tears burst forth:
"How sorrowful is woman's lot!" she cried.
"How sternly fate will deal with all of us!
Creator, why are you so mean and cruel,
blighting green days and fading rosy cheeks?
In life she played the wife to all the world,
alas, to end in hell without a man!
Where are they now, who once shared her embrace?
Where are they now, who once vied for her charms?
Since no one deigns to cast a glance her way,
while I am here I'll light some incense sticks
to mark the day I came across her grave.
Perhaps down by the Yellow Springs[12] she'll know."
    Kieu prayed in mumbled tones, then she knelt down
to make a few low bows before the tomb.
Dusk gathered on the patch of dying weeds.
Reed tassels shivered in the passing breeze.
She pulled a pin out of her hair and graved
four lines of cut-off verse[13] on a tree's bark.
Lost in tranced reverie, without a word,
she tarried there and would not take her leave.
The cloud upon her face grew darker yet—
as sorrow ebbed and flowed, tears dripped or streamed.
    "Sister, you truly make me laugh," said Van,
"wasting your tears on one long dead and gone!"
Kieu answered: "Since the universe began,
when have fair women known a happy fate?
As I see her lie there, it hurts to think
what will become of me in later life."
    "That's a fine way to talk!" protested Quan.
"It grates the ear to hear you put yourself
in Dam Tien's plight. Let's shun this morbid air.

Day's fading and there's still a long way home."
   "When one who shines in talent dies," said Kieu,
"the body perishes, but not the soul.
Perhaps in her I've found a kindred heart.
If so I'll wait, and soon she will appear!"
   Before they could respond to what she said,
a whirlwind rose from nowhere, raged and raved,
scattering the tender buds and shaking trees
and leaving whiffs of perfume in the air.
Now following the path the whirlwind took,
they plainly saw fresh footprints on the moss.
They stared at one another, terror-struck.
"You listened to my prayer, Dam Tien!" Kieu cried.
"To join our kindred hearts our paths have crossed,
and beyond life and death sisters have met!"
   Thus manifest to sight the ghost had come—
to her quatrain Kieu added words of thanks.
A poet's feelings flowed and brooked no bounds:
upon the bark she wrote an old-style poem.[14]

   To leave or stay—they all were wavering still
when drawing near they heard the sound of bells.
They saw a youthful scholar come their way
astride a colt he rode with slackened rein.
He carried half a bagful of love poems,
and page-boys tended him, tagging behind.
His frisky horse had a coat white as snow.
His gown commingled tints of grass and sky.
No sooner had he spied them from afar
than he dismounted and walked straight to them.
In his embroidered shoes he trod the grass,
a figure shining like ruby and jade.
Young Vuong stepped forth to greet one that he knew
while two shy maidens hid behind the flowers.

He came from somewhere not so far away—
Kim Trong, a scion of the noblest stock.
From a clan blessed with talent and with wealth,
nature and nurture both had formed his mind.
Looks and manners set him above the crowd.
At home he led the gracious life of books,
and in the world he gave with open hand.
Since birth he had lived always in these parts—
he and young Vuong had gone to the same school.
    His neighbors' fame had spread and reached his ears:
two beauties locked in a Bronze Sparrow Tower![15]
But, as if hills and streams had barred the way,
he had long sighed and dreamt of them in vain.
How lucky then, at this time of new leaves,
to wander off and find his sought-for flowers!
Afar he caught a glimpse of Van and Kieu:
orchid in spring, chrysanthemum in fall,
both were enchanting—each in her own season!
    Beautiful girl and talented young man—
what their hearts felt, their eyes still dared not say.
They stood entranced, half waking, half in dream—
they could not stay, nor would they soon depart.
The dusk of sunset prompted gloomy thoughts—
he left, and longingly she watched him go.
Below, still pure and clear, the brook flowed on,
and by the bridge the willows swished their leaves.

    When Kieu got home behind her flowered drapes,
the sun had set, the curfew gong had rung.
At the window the moon was peering in.
It splashed ripples of gold across the waves,
projected dark tree shadows on the yard.
A camellia drooped east, toward the next house.
As dewdrops fell, the spring branch bent and bowed.

Alone, in silence, Kieu gazed at the moon,
her heart a raveled coil of fears and hopes:
"How could that girl have come to such a pass?
A wretched end to such a glittering life!
And why should I have met him on my way
unless fate meant some tie between us two?"
Her bosom heaved in turmoil, she poured forth
a wondrous lyric fraught with all she felt.

A tilting moon shone starkly through the blinds.
Kieu leaned against a rail and fell asleep.
Now out of nowhere there appeared a girl
with worldly glamor joined to childlike grace:
face washed with dewdrops, body clad in snow,
and hovering feet, two golden lotus blooms.[16]
With joy Kieu hailed the stranger, asking her:
"Did you stray here from the Peach Blossom Source?"[17]
"We two are sister souls," the other said.
"Have you forgotten? We met just today!
My chilly resting-place lies west of here,
above a gurgling brook, beneath a bridge.
Who else but you has stooped to notice me
and strew poetic jewels on my grave?
I showed them to the League Chief[18] and was told
your name was there, in the Book of the Damned;
that is the fruit of deeds in your past lives.
You are no stranger—you and I belong
to the same League and ride in the same boat.
Here are ten subjects that the Chief just set.
Once more pray work your magic with a brush!"

Kieu did as ordered. With a nymphlike grace
and lightning strokes of brush, she wrote ten songs.
Dam Tien read them and marveled to herself:
"Rich-wrought embroidery from a heart of gold!
In the Book of the Damned, which one of us

could surpass her and carry off the prize?"

On the threshold the ghost had turned to leave,
but Kieu would hold her back and talk some more.
A sudden gust of wind disturbed the blinds:
Kieu woke and knew it all had been a dream.
She looked around: no one was to be seen,
though hints of perfume lingered in the air.

The night was deepening. Lonely, distraught,
Kieu viewed the way ahead with doubt and fear.
A storm-tossed rose, a duckweed cut adrift—
such was her future, all she'd ever be.
Her inmost feelings rose, wave upon wave—
again and yet again she broke and cried.

Her sobs were carried through the figured drapes.
Wakened, her mother asked: "What troubles you
that you still stir and fret at dead of night,
and tears rain down on your pear-blossom face?"[19]
"This young and foolish daughter," answered Kieu,
"has caused you two nothing but pain and care!
Today, while walking, I found Dam Tien's grave—
then in a dream, tonight, I saw her here.
She said that I, like her, am of the Damned,
and asked me to write verse upon that theme.
As I interpret what the dream portends,
my life in days ahead won't come to much!"
Her mother said: "Are dreams such solid grounds
that you will build thereon a tale of woe?"

Kieu tried to heed her mother's chiding voice,
but soon her tears arose and flowed again.
Outside, an oriole began to chirp—
a willow catkin dropped, to drift next door.
By now the moonbeams fell aslant the eaves.
Kieu stayed alone—alone with her own grief.

* * *

How strange the race of lovers! Try as one will,
one can't unsnarl their hearts' entangled threads.
   Back in his room, surrounded by his books,
Kim could not shut Kieu's image from his mind.
He drained the cup of gloom—it filled anew;
one day away from her: three autumns long.
Now silken curtains veiled her like a cloud—
he moved in the world's dust but lived in dreams.
As the moon waned and the lamp sputtered low,
his face yearned for her face, his heart for hers.
The study-room grew still and cold as ice—
brushes lay dry, lute strings hung loose on frets.
A rustling breeze played music on the blinds.
He vainly kindled incense and drank tea,
craving her scent and missing love's sweet taste.
Unless the heavens destined her for him,
why had the temptress come and teased his eyes?
Racked with desire, he pictured place and girl:
he rushed back to the scene where they had met.
He could still view the meadow, lush and green,
and the unmuddied stream—but nothing more.
The breeze at twilight stirred a mood of woe—
the sedges shook their heads in seeming taunts.
Fancy supplies all that the mind forgets—
in search of Kieu, he dashed toward the Blue Bridge.[20]
   Locked gates and high steep walls enshrined the girl.
No stream to float the Crimson Leaf of love![21]
No passage for the bluebird to bear news![22]
The willows' scattered locks of silk drooped down.
An oriole mocked him upon the branch.
All doors were shut. He found no sign of Kieu
near the front steps bestrewn with fallen flowers.
   He stood and waited for a long, long time.
Then he walked to the rear, and there he saw—

a house to let! The owner was away—
a merchant seeking wealth in heathen climes.

Young Kim, as student, came to rent the place—
he settled in with brushes, books, and lute.
An ideal site with rock garden and trees,
and with a well-named porch—Kingfisher View![23]
"Her very name in vivid golden[24] script!"
exulted he. "The handwriting of fate!"
He opened up the window just a crack,
and daily peeped over the Eastern wall.
The fairy grotto, though, remained sealed tight:
no rosy nymph was flitting in or out.

Since he left home to dwell in a strange place,
twice on its rounds the moon had come and gone.
Then, on a balmy day, across the wall,
he thought he saw her stroll beneath the trees.
He dropped his lute, smoothed out his gown, rushed forth:
the breeze still held her scent, but she had fled.

As he paced round the wall, his eyes caught sight
of a gold hairpin stuck on a peach branch.
He quickly reached for it and took it home.
"How did it leave her room to come this way?"
he asked. "For it is hers, and fate has willed
that it should thus have fallen in my hands!"
Now sleepless, he admired and stroked the pin
still faintly redolent of sandalwood.

Next day, as dawn's mist cleared, she went back there
to search along the wall with anxious eyes.
He, all the while, had been biding his chance.
Across the wall he spoke to test her heart:
"Out of the blue this pin has come to me.
I'd like to know who may claim it by right.
The pearl wants to go back—but where's Ho-p'u?"[25]

Now Kieu's response came from the other side:

"I thank you for returning what I lost.
A pin is not worth much, but beyond price
is a man's sense of what is right and wrong."

Kim said to her: "We two have lived so near,
we should not be mere strangers but close friends.
You lost a whiff of scent—and I found you!
For this one chance what torments I have borne!
For this one minute I have waited months!
Please stay and hear the secret of my heart!"

He hurried home to fetch a few more things:
two golden bracelets and a square of silk.
By ladder he could climb over the wall.
She was the one that he had glimpsed that day!
Embarrassed, she maintained a shy reserve—
while he looked in her face she dropped her head.

He told her: "Ever since we met by chance,
in secret I have yearned and pined for you!
I've wasted to the bone as I gave up
all hopes of living on to see this day.
For months my soul has dwelt among the clouds.
I've hugged my forlorn hope like that poor lad
who hugged a pillar waiting for his love.[26]
But now you're facing me! I beg to know—
will your mirror shine on my worthless self?"

Kieu faltered and demurred before she said:
"Our ways are simple and as pure as snow,
the ways of folk who eat cabbage and cress.
When it comes to the Crimson Leaf of love
or the Red Thread of marriage,[27] it's not I
but my parents who will say yes or no.
You deign to care for me, but I'm too young,
too ignorant to dare engage my troth."

"It blows one day and rains the next," he said.
"How often will a springtime chance recur?

If you don't listen to my prayer of love,
you'll hurt me—yet what will it profit you?
Let's swear the word that binds. Then, later on,
with proper rites I shall approach your clan.
Should Heaven disappoint me, wreck my hopes,
I'll throw away a life in its first bloom!
Should you reject my plea with heartless scorn,
my love and zeal will have labored for naught!"
    She listened, lulled with sweetest melody—
it charmed her senses, he bemused her eyes.
"New though our friendship be," she said at last,
"how can my heart resist your heart's behest?
Since in your noble soul I've found my place,
I shall engrave my troth on stone and bronze!"
    Her words untied a knot within his breast.
He gave her back the pin in a red scarf.
"Now I am bound to you for life," he said.
"Accept this little token of my love."
With her embroidered handkerchief she had
her sunflower fan—the flower of constancy.[28]
She traded them at once for pin and gifts.
    Swearing a solemn oath to seal their pact,
they heard a noise and voices from the rear.
In a flurry of falling leaves and flowers,
she fled back to her chamber, he to his.

    The stone and gold had touched. But from then on,
as their love grew, so deeper grew their gloom.
The Hsiang River ran dry—a trickle now:
he waited at the source, she at the mouth.[29]
The wall rose like a mountain range between,
and words of love could not go back and forth.
    As windy days and moonlit nights whirled round,
red decreased, green increased, and spring was past.

A birthday feast fell due in Mother's clan.
Both parents then, with Van and Quan in tow,
departed richly dressed and bearing gifts
to wish their kinsman health and happy life.

In the deserted house Kieu was alone.
"Today's the day to see my love!" she thought.
She set out things in season—meats and fruits—
then toward the wall she nimbly bent her steps.
She gave a faint-voiced call across the flowers:
he was already there awaiting her.

He spoke words of reproach: "Your ardor's cooled!
Since then you've let love's incense burn to ash!
But I have only sighed and pined the while,
and grief has touched my hair with streaks of gray!"
"Wind's held me up, rain's kept me back!" she said.
"I've hurt your feelings much against my will.
Today I'm home all by myself—I've come
to make amends and repay love for love."

She slid along the rocks, then she went round
to reach a gate at the wall's farther end.
Her sleeve rolled up, she raised the locking bar—
the way was clear to the Garden of Love.

At long last, face to face aglow with joy!
After the bows and greetings, side by side
they walked together to his study-room,
while mingling tender words and solemn vows.

A rack for brushes and a tube for poems
stood on his desk. Above, there hung a sketch—
a pine tree freshly drawn with brush and ink.
Frost-bitten and wind-battered, it looked real!
The more she gazed, the more it sprang to life.
"It's something I dashed off just now," he said.
"To give it worth may I beg from your brush
some kind comments?" Hand dancing like a nymph

and swift as lashing wind or driving rain,
she wrote a few quatrains atop the pine.
"Your magic works to conjure pearls and gems!"
he cried in praise. "Poetesses of old
like Pan and Hsieh[30] could not have bettered this!
I should have lived a saintly life before
to merit my good fortune at this time!"
    "I've dared to read your noble face," Kieu said.
"You'll cross the Golden Portal and wear jade.[31]
But what's my destiny? A May fly's wing!
Will Heaven care to smooth things down for us?
I still remember—in my childhood days,
a seer observed my features and foretold:
'When charms and gifts shine forth from a girl's face,
she'll lead a life of woes—an artist's life.'
I view your lot, then look back on my own:
two worlds at odds, how could they blend as one?"
    "Yet after all, we two have met!" he said.
"Man's will can often vanquish Heaven's whim!
But if a cruel fate should sever us,
I'll take a sword and end my hopeless life!"
Their souls' recesses yielded words of love—
the cup of spring was sipped, and young hearts leapt.
    A happy day is shorter than a span.
The Western hills had swallowed half the sun.
Kieu could no longer stay—she bowed her leave
to hurry home and watch the empty house.

    Word from her parents was awaiting Kieu:
the feast went on, they would not soon be back.
She dropped the silken curtain at the door,
then crossed the garden in dark night, alone.
A dappled moon was peeping through the leaves,
and through the drapes she glimpsed a fitful light.

The student at his desk had just dozed off,
reclining half awake and half asleep.
The patter of her steps disturbed his rest
as she approached him in the moonlit dusk.
Was this a spring night's dream? He thought he saw
the Nymph of Love come to him from Mount Chia[32]
while he dwelt on Mount Shen[33] among the gods.

"Upon a lonesome, darkened path," she said,
"for love of you I found my way to you.
Now we stand face to face—but who can tell
we won't wake up and learn it's been a dream?"

Conceive the young man's joy! He swift replaced
the candle and refilled the incense bowl.
They wrote a pledge of love and, with a knife,
they cut in two a tress of her long hair.
Then, while the moon was watching from the skies,
with one voice both pronounced their sacred oath.
Both shared the secrets of their heart of hearts—
both pledged their union in their very souls.

They sipped a nectar-wine from cups of jade.
Her sash of silk gave off a heady scent.
His crystal screen enclosed her mirrored form.
"The breeze is cool, the moon is clear," he sighed.
"But in my heart still burns a secret thirst.
I've yet to cross the Blue Bridge as a groom:
I fear that my request may give offense."
"The Crimson Leaf has given us its word,"
she said. "And the Red Thread now binds us two,
for we have traded vows that seal our troth.
Do not ask me to trifle with our love
and treat it as a game of moon and flowers.[34]
Grant this and I'll deny you nothing else!"

"You are well-famed as lute-player," he said.
"Like Chung Tzu-ch'i[35] I've longed to hear you play."

"It's no great art, my luting," she replied.
"But if you so command, I must submit."
In the back porch there hung his moon-shaped lute—[36]
he hurried to present it in both hands,
at eyebrow's height. "My petty skill," she cried,
"is causing you more trouble than it's worth!"

She touched the strings in turn, both high and low,
and tuned them to all five tones of the scale.
Now she began to play. A battle scene—
oh how they clashed and clanged, Han and Ch'u[37] swords!
The Ssu-ma tune, *A Phoenix Seeks His Mate*—[38]
it sounded like an outburst of pure grief.
Then Hsi K'ang's masterpiece, *Kuang-ling*,[39] was heard:
it rushed on like a stream or flew like clouds.
Next came what Chao-chün[40] played—she mourned her
                                        Prince
and all her kinsfolk she must leave behind
as she crossed the Great Wall to wed a Hun!
Sheer notes like flights of herons rustling by,
or somber tones like tumbling waterfalls . . .
A pace now languid as an idle breeze,
now fast and furious as a pouring rain . . .

The flickering candle flared and dimmed by turns—
and there he sat like one in gloomy trance.
Now with bent head he'd lean upon his knees,
now he'd contract his brow in anguished pain.
"How masterly your touch!" he cried at last.
"But it reveals such bitterness within!
Why do you choose to play in minor keys
that wring your heart and torture other souls?"
"It's just a quirk of nature," she replied.
"As pleases Heaven, one's born sad or gay.
But I shall note your golden words, their truth—
I hope some day my humor will improve."

A fragrant rose, she sparkled in full bloom,
and in full flood desire suffused his eyes.
As he succumbed to surging waves of lust,
his wooing showed some signs of unrestraint.
   "Of love don't make a game!" she chided him.
"Please stay away from me and let me speak.
On the peach tree I am too plain a bud
to venture fending off the Bluebird's quest.
But I'm your promised wife—and for her man
a bride must keep her soul and body pure.
If like the maids in those mulberry-groves
on the P'u River banks[41] I misbehaved,
would you still sue for such a wench's hand?
If we reached out and seized the moment's thrill,
we'd damage in one day a lifelong trust.
Of all the lovers sung by ancient bards,
which other pair could equal Ts'ui and Chang?[42]
And yet excess destroyed their plighted troth:
she humored all his whims and killed their love.
As wing to wing and limb to limb they lay,[43]
contempt already lurked inside their hearts.
In time love's fire went out. They broke the vows
that in the Western Chamber both had sworn—
their love, unblessed with wedlock, died in shame.
If I don't cast the shuttle to resist[44]
and guilt should haunt our lives, who should be blamed?
Why force your wish on a shy flower so soon?
Before I die, you'll one day get your due!"
   The voice of sober wisdom gained his ear,
and tenfold his regard for her increased.
Then, as the moon grew faint along the eaves,
a calling voice was heard outside the gate.
Kieu ran back to her chamber, and young Kim
rushed through the yard where peach trees were in bloom.

49

Young Kim unlocked the entrance gate to find
a servant with a message from his clan.
It said his father's brother had passed on,
and the remains were now to be brought home—
from far-away Liao-yang.[1] Kim was at once
to hurry there and lead the funeral.

Who can describe his shock? Without delay,
he stole to Kieu's back porch. He broke the news,
explaining how one death that struck a clan
could also pull two lovers far apart:

"We've scarcely shared two moments by ourselves!
We've had no chance to tie the marriage knot!
But it glows still, the moon that we swore by:
no absence will estrange true hearts in love.
A thousand miles between us for three years!
It will be long before our sorrow ends.
Care dearly for yourself, my gold and jade,
that over there my soul may know some rest."

She heard him speak, her thoughts all in a snarl.
Now sobbingly she told him how she felt:
"Why does the Wedlock God obstruct us so?
The joy of union we have never known—
but we can tell how much it hurts to part!
Together we did swear a sacred oath:
I will grow gray and wither—not my love.
I'll wait for you if it takes years and years.
In secret I shall grieve as, in my mind,
I'll see you push your way through winds and frosts.
To you I pledged my heart and soul for life.
No one but you shall ever be my man
and hear me play my lute aboard his boat.[2]
As long as hills and rivers shall endure,
you too will think of me and will return!"

They lingered hand in hand—they could not part.
But now the sun stood high above the roof.
Kim left, sore wrenched by every step he took,
and still in tears looked back to say good-bye.
Horse saddled and bags packed, he hurried off—
the lovers split their grief and parted ways.

Strange scenes and landscapes met his mournful eyes.
The cuckoos, perched on branches, cried and cried—
geese winging homeward wrinkled heaven's edge.
Through wind and rain the lonely traveler dragged
a heart burdened with love, day after day.

There Kieu remained, her back against the porch,
her feelings raveled like a skein of silk.
Through latticework unseeingly she stared
at wisps of smoke far off—a rose adrift,
its colors dulled, a willow gaunt and pale.
Distracted, she was walking back and forth
when from the feast her family returned.

They had no time to settle down and chat,
for constables came rushing from all sides.
   Armed to the teeth with knives and wooden staves,
they madly ran around, more beasts than men.
They clapped a cangue on father and on son,
and with a single rope they trussed both up.
Then, like bluebottles buzzing through the place,
they broke workbaskets and handlooms to bits;
they grabbed at goods and chattels, odds and ends,
picking all corners clean to fill their sacks.
   What crime had they committed, these good folk?
Who had trumped up the charge and sprung the trap?
(Upon inquiry, it was later learned
the plaintiff was some knave who sold raw silk.)
A fear-struck household was turned upside down.
The air was rent with cries of innocence
and shrill protests against iniquity.
All day, the victims groveled and crouched low,
pleading to stone-deaf ears. Father and son
were beaten black-and-blue, then to a beam
their feet were tied—they dangled there, heads down.
The piteous sight would have softened a rock—
their features twisted in dire pain and fear.
Now only Heaven could redress this wrong—
alas, just Heaven ruled so far away!
The myrmidons put in a good day's work—
for money they would maim and murder, too.

   Kieu had to save her kin, her flesh and blood.
When evil strikes, one bows to circumstance.
When one must weigh and choose between one's love
and filial duty, which will turn the scale?
Kieu brushed aside her solemn vows to Kim—
she'd pay a daughter's debt before all else.

Resolved on what to do, she spoke her mind:
"Hands off my father, please! I'll sell myself
and ransom him."
                        There was old Chung, a scribe,
who felt compassion that belied his trade.
He was impressed with a true daughter's love,
and it grieved him to see Kieu sorely tried.
He reckoned up how much it all would cost
to bribe and pave this way or clear that path:
three hundred liang of silver! He'd obtain
the prisoner's release, but she was told
to find the sum within two or three days.
O pity her, so young and innocent!
Misfortune overtook her like a storm.
To part with him she loved would be like death—
but life was nothing now, no matter love.
Does a raindrop decide where it will fall?
From spring a leaf of grass receives its green:[3]
to her father she owed the debt of life.
    Matchmakers were advised of Kieu's intent—
fleet rumor cast the news to the four winds.
Now an old woman, living in those parts,
came to present a man from out of town.
When asked he gave his name as "Scholar Ma—
of the Imperial University."[4]
He claimed his home to be "Lin-ch'ing, near here."
Past forty, he had left his youth behind,
but still he wore smart clothes and a smooth face.
The master led his noisy suite of men
and was escorted to the inner rooms.
As he ensconced himself in the best chair,
the broker went and urged the girl to come.
    Crushed by her kinsfolk's woe and her own grief,
Kieu crossed the doorsill, and her tears fell free—

a rose in bud confronted winds and dews.
The sight of flowers brought blushes to her cheeks,
and mirrors showed her face full flushed with shame.
The crone caressed her hair and held her hand—
Kieu silent sat, an aster in late fall,
a spray of apricot so thin and wan.
    She was sized up and judged for looks and skills.
They made her play some chords upon the lute.
They made her write some verses on a fan.
Her many charms were tasted and enjoyed.
Well pleased, the man set out to clinch a deal:
    "I came to the Blue Bridge seeking a bride.
I'd like to know the price I am to pay."
"She's worth her weight in gold!" the broker crowed.
"But then her folk are caught in a tight spot—
they'll throw themselves upon your charity."
They haggled and they haggled, then both sides
agreed upon three hundred and some liang.
All was smooth sailing once the word was said.
To seal the contract man and girl exchanged
betrothal cards bearing birthdays and names.
They set a date to pay the bridal price
when, yoked, they could go home to wedded bliss.
The man had cash, and cash set things aright.
Old Chung, the scribe, was asked to intercede.
Into his custody old Vuong was freed.
    Poor father and poor daughter, face to face!
He looked at her and bled within. He cried:
"You raise a daughter hoping that, one day,
she'll tie the Red Silk Thread with some good man,
she'll toss the ball into some worthy hands.[5]
O Heaven, why inflict such woes on us?
Who slandered us to tear our home apart?
I would not mind the ax for these old bones,

but cannot bear to see my daughter harmed!
Death now or later happens only once—
I'd sooner die than live this agony!"
    And thereupon the father sobbed anew
and wildly banged his head against a wall.
They rushed to stop him. In a soothing voice,
Kieu tried to reason with the desperate man:
"What is this daughter worth who has not yet
repaid one whit for all your cares and pains?
I feel ashamed not to have done like Ying[6]
and petitioned His Majesty for you.
Then should I also fail to rival Li[7]
who, to redeem her father, sold herself?
As he grows old, a father's like a tree—
he carries and supports many a branch.
If you don't see your way to let me go,
I fear a windstorm will destroy us all.
Sacrifice me alone and save our home:
one flower will fall, but green the tree will stay.
Whatever happens, I will bear my lot.
Just think of me as one nipped in the bud—
let no more wild ideas run through your head!
You'll hurt your loved ones and your very self."
She talked good sense—it sank into his ears.
They gazed upon each other and they wept.
    But outside Scholar Ma had come again.
They signed the contract—he delivered cash.
A wanton god, the Old Man of the Moon,[8]
how randomly he knots his wedlock ties!
    With money held in hand it's no great trick
to change men's hearts and turn black into white.
Old Chung, the scribe, did all he could to help—
once gifts were offered up, the case was closed.

                    * * *

Now while a lull succeeded stormy times,
the bridal day and hour drew on apace.
Alone, Kieu sat beside her midnight lamp
with tear-washed gown and sorrow-withered hair:
   "For good or ill, I shall accept my fate.
But it grieves me to think of my true love.
Oh how he toiled and strove to win my heart!
Yet as he pledged his faith, he wrecked his life.
The cup we drank from then has hardly dried
when I now break my oath and play him false.
In far-off Liao, little does he suspect
our love has been destroyed by my own hands.
And all the lovers' vows we two exchanged,
alas, will come to nothing in this life.
But in some afterlife, yet bound by them,
I'll be reborn a beast to make amends!
Until the debt of love is paid in full,
my heart of love shall not melt in the grave!"
   Dark thoughts kept turning over in her mind.
The oil had all burned out—tears soaked her scarf.
Van, who had just awaked from a sweet dream,
came to the lamp and tenderly observed:
"Heaven's involved design of flux and change
has chosen you to bear our woes alone.
Is that why you've stayed up the livelong night?
Or is some private hurt still vexing you?"
   "My heart's near bursting with a stifled cry,"
said Kieu, "for it's still struggling in love's webs.
I feel ashamed to part my lips and tell,
but if I don't I'll have betrayed his faith.
I'll beg one thing of you, my sister—but
let me bow first to you in gratitude.
In mid career I have destroyed my troth—
I pray you, Van, to mend the shattered bits.

After I met Kim Trong on that spring stroll,
I gave him my own fan to pledge my love—
we drank of the same cup to swear our vows.
But wind and tide have swept it all away,
for how can love and duty both prevail?
Ahead of you still lie your fairest days.
Belovèd sister, hear the call of blood
and, in my stead, redeem my pledge to Kim.
My flesh will rot, my bones will turn to dust—
yet down by the Nine Springs[9] I'll smile and breathe
the fragrance of your dual happiness.
Keep these gold bracelets and this written pledge
as proofs and tokens of our common love.
When he and you become husband and wife,
I trust you won't forget this luckless girl.
By then I'll have been gone—here are two things
to keep my memory: this lute of his
and this incense we burned taking our oath.
Someday, if you should chance to tune the lute
and light the incense, cast a glance outside:
you'll see the grass and leaves stir in the breeze
and know that your poor sister has come back.
My body will have crumbled into earth—
yet haunted in my soul by my sworn oath,
I shall return to fulfill all my vows!
In the Dark Realm I'll not be seen or heard—
please sprinkle water from a cup for me
to cool the thirst of one so wronged by fate.
My plighted troth in bits and pieces now—
a mirror cracked, a hairpin snapped in two!
Past all expression, how I cherish him!
Through you I'll send my humblest bows to him.
Ah me, that's all there is to our brief love.
Why have I drawn a lot as gray as dust?

57

This flower will fall and down the stream will float!
O my belovèd Kim, as of today
I'm forced to break the sacred oath we took!"
    This said, as blood rushed from her face, she swooned—
her breathing flagged, her hands turned cold as death.
The parents were aroused from their deep sleep.
A tumult stirred the household as pell-mell
all hurried in and out to fetch some cure.
The girl came back to life and cried again.
When she was asked why she behaved that way,
she sobbed and sobbed and could not find her voice.
Van whispered something in their father's ear,
showing gold bracelets and the written pledge.
    "For me you broke your plighted troth!" he sighed.
"But Van shall honor it on your behalf.
From amber who has torn the mustard seed,[10]
and from its magnet ripped away the pin,
that like duckweed and cloud you'll float and drift?
Believe me, though: your wish shall be my will.
A stone may break, but not my word to you!"
    Kieu made a deep obeisance, then she said:
"If you help Van make good my pledge to Kim,
I'll gladly settle for my fate—a slave's.
Content, I'll live and die on alien soil."

    Her sorrow soared—higher than words could reach—
when on the Southern tower the watchman tolled
the knell of night with hurried beats of drum.
A sedan-chair appeared soon at the gate,
with flutes and lutes, to wrest the bride away.
She grieved to go, they grieved to stay behind—
tears drenched the steps as parting tugged at hearts.
    Across a twilit sky spread lowering clouds.
Grass drooped and branches bowed beneath the dew.

Ma led the maiden to a roadside inn,
then left her there alone, within four walls.
Both shame and dread contended for her soul—
brooding over her lot, she grieved and grieved.
From sun and rain she had guarded for Kim
a beauteous flower now lying in vile hands.
"Would I had known I'd fall so low!" she moaned.
"I would have let my true love pick the peach.
I fenced my garden well from the East wind![11]
Why fail him then only to rue it now?
If I should meet with him again, someday,
what hope for happiness is left to us?
If I indeed was born to float and drift,
how can I then go on with such a life?"
    Before her on a table lay a knife—
she stole it and concealed it in her scarf.
"The tide may reach my feet," she thought. "If so,
this knife will serve to settle with my fate."
    The autumn night wore on. All by herself,
Kieu hovered in a haze of wake and dream.
How little did she know about the groom!
Ma long had patronized the haunts of lust.
Much whoring and some strokes of blackest luck
had ruined him: the scholar settled down
in harlotdom to work for bed and board.
Now in a brothel languished a Dame Tu
whose once rich charms were taxed by creeping age.
Upon one common ground two met and merged—
she swapped her sawdust for his bitter melon,[12]
and thus a cheat was set to catch a cheat.
They pooled assets and funds and opened shop
to sell their painted dolls twelve months a year.
He scoured country and town for 'concubines'
to whom the bawd would teach the trade of love.

One's fortune, good or ill, is heaven-sent.
In Kieu a perverse fate had found its butt.
Alas, the maiden was so young and fair!
A rose had dropped into a huckster's boat!
The pimp had caught his prey, baiting a trap
with paltry wedding gifts and slapdash rites.
   "The maid lies in my power!" thought Scholar Ma.
"He waves the flag who holds it in his hand![13]
The more I view her charms, the more I rave!
Celestial hue! Unearthly scent! Her price
is far above all gold and no mistake!
When she gets there, to pluck the maiden bud
princes and gentlefolk will push and shove.
She'll bring at least three hundred or about
what I have paid for her. And after that,
all she will earn is profit, net and clear.
But when a tidbit dangles at your mouth,
should you protect the money you invest
or should you eat what Heaven has served up?
A peach divine within a mortal's grasp!
Well, let me bend the branch and pick the fruit
and gobble it to make my life complete!
How many flower collectors in the world
can really tell one rose from the next rose?
Juice from pomegranate skin and cockscomb blood,
in proper mixture, lend the pristine look—
in the half-light, a yokel will be fooled!
Though less than new, no less money she'll fetch.
If the old girl finds out and makes a scene,
I'll bear it like a man, upon my knees!
In any case, it's a long journey home—
if I don't go near her, I'll look suspect."
   Alas, a pure camellia was defiled—
she let the bee know his way in and out!

A storm of bestial lust broke forth—it raged
against the virgin scent, the flawless jewel.
To nightmare turned her dream of nuptial bliss—
then she woke up to lie there, by herself,
and tears of silent grief poured down like rain.
She hated him and loathed herself as much:
"What breed or kind is he that smells so foul?
My smirched body now hides a woman's shame!
What hope remains for me after all this?
A life that's come to this is life no more!"

By turns she moaned and cursed her destiny.
She took the knife, ready to kill herself.
But then she weighed and balanced in her mind:
"My kinsfolk are at stake, not I alone.
If anything should happen to me now,
the law will intervene and work their doom.
Who knows? My plight could mend with passing time—
if not, I'll later set my date with death!"

While still she pondered what she ought to do,
the cock's crow sounded from outside the wall—
the daybreak horn on the watchtower soon blared.
So Scholar Ma made haste to scamper off.
Oh how it rent the heart, the time to leave,
when horse began to trot and wheels to jolt!

Ten miles beyond the city, at a stop,
the father bade them farewell with a feast.
Outside, the host and guests were drinking healths.
Inside, mother and bride were huddled now,
gazing upon each other through their tears.
In mother's ear Kieu whispered all her doubts:

"I am a girl, so helpless, to my shame—
when could I ever pay a daughter's debts?
We're victims in a world all twisted round,
where mud to water turns, water to mud.

From this moment I'll leave with you my heart.
To judge by what I've noticed these few days,
I fear my life is in a swindler's hands.
When we got there, he left me by myself,
and with a hangdog look he slunk away.
He mumbles and he stammers, face to face.
His men show nothing but contempt for him.
He lacks the ease and grace of cultured folk,
seeming more like a trader on close watch.
It must be said—your daughter's fate is sealed!
Far, far away from home they'll dig her grave!"
The mother had no sooner heard these words
than she cried out for justice—a shrill wail
that rose and would pierce through heaven itself.

　　Even before the parting cup was drained,
Ma rushed outside and urged the coach to leave.
His daughter's future weighed upon his mind,
so by the saddle Vuong implored the groom:
"Because disaster struck our home, my child
is now reduced to serving you as slave.
Among strange faces, at the world's far end,
she'll pass her lonesome days in rain or shine.
You'll be the lofty oak—when the snows fall,
please let the vine depend on you for warmth!"
Whereat the groom replied with a low bow:
"The Red Silk Thread has closely tied our feet.
Witness the sun and moon—if I break faith,
may Heaven's sword of vengeance smite me down!"

　　With a loud clatter, swiftly as the wind,
the coach took off in whirls of ocher dust.
Kieu's parents wiped their tears and strained their eyes
to watch her fade from sight. And daily now,
on the horizon they would fix their gaze.

Kieu traveled far, far into the unknown.
Frosts streaked the bridges, clouds enwrapped the woods.
Reeds thrilled and huddled in the cold North wind.
The autumn mourned for her and her alone.
A midnight path—a sky of hush and mist.
The moon, a witness to her vows, cried shame.
From tier to tier of jasper flecked with reds
birds sent their calls—"Home! Home!" they told her heart.
She crossed strange streams, climbed mountains with no
                                        names.
The moon waxed full again—Lin-tzu[1] was reached.
    The coach pulled up outside the gate. Straightway,
a woman parted curtains and emerged.
She struck one at first glance with her pale skin—
but what did she gorge on to gain such bulk?
Swinging her hips she came and greeted Kieu:
Kieu at her bidding meekly stepped indoors.
    On one side, there were girls with penciled brows—

and on the other four or five gay blades.
Between, festooned with wreaths of incense smoke,
there hung on high the image of a god—
the White-Browed God. For in all Green Pavilions,
(or bawdyhouses) custom so prescribed—
he was worshipped as patron saint by whores
and offered flowers and incense night and day.
When luck forsook a girl and trade was slow,
in front of him she'd doff her shirt and skirt.
Stripped to the skin, she would intone a prayer
and burn a votive bunch of incense sticks;
then on the altar she would place fresh flowers;
the faded ones she'd take to line her bed—
and presto, bees would swarm from miles around!

Confused and lost, Kieu knew no other course,
so she knelt down as told. The bawd now prayed:
"May fortune bless this house and business thrive
on nights of mirth, on days of revelry!
May all the men be smitten by this maid
and all come bustling, panting after her!
Let them swamp her with messages of love
and throng to her by both front door and back!"
That made no sense to Kieu's bewildered ears—
and all about this place she found quite odd.

Once the observance had been duly done,
the bawd installed herself upon a couch.
She ordered Kieu: "Kneel and bow to Mama!
Then go and do the same for your Pa there!"

"Condemned by fate to exile," said the girl,
"I've hugged my humble lot as concubine.
But you take me for something else, it seems—
a swallow has become an oriole!
I don't know what I am, I must admit.
With wedding gifts and nuptial rites and all,

we were made man and wife—we've lived as such.
Now it turns out our roles and ranks have changed.
May I beg you to clear it up for me?"
    The woman heard the tale and learned the truth.
Her devils, fiends, and demons all broke loose.
"It's plain what happened, what they did!" she shrieked.
"You, strumpet, stole my man for your own use!
I sent him off for girls to bring back here
and train as hostesses—that's how we eat!
But the false-hearted knave, the beastly swine
had his damn itch and messed around with you!
Now that the cloth has lost its glaze and starch,
there goes to hell the money I put up!
You little slut, they sold you to me here,
and in my house you go by my house rules.
When that old lecher stooped to his foul tricks,
why did you fail to slap him in the face?
Why did you just lie there and take it all?
Young as you were, did you already rut?
I must teach you how I lay down the law!"
    She grabbed a whip, about to pounce and lash.
"Heaven and earth bear witness!" Kieu cried out.
"My life's as good as lost since I left home!
What now remains of it to save and hold?"
At once she drew the weapon from her sleeve—
O horror, she found heart to kill herself!
The bawd looked on aghast as the girl stabbed.
Ah me, were all her talents and her charms
to leave this earth, dissevered by a knife?
    The wrong Kieu suffered was soon noised abroad,
and curious idlers came to fill the house.
The senseless girl was lying there near death—
trembling with fear, the bawd just stood and stared.
Then Kieu was carried to the western wing—

a doctor was called in to save her life.

Kieu's ties to the Dust World were not yet cut.
She dreamed a girl appeared hard by her side
and murmured: "Kieu! Your Karma's still undone.
How can you shirk your debt of grief to fate?
You yet have to play out your woman's role.
You wish to flee, but will Heaven permit?
Stay and live out the life of a frail reed!
Ch'ien-t'ang River[2] shall find us two again!"

With balms and salves applied the whole day through,
Kieu then awakened from her deathlike sleep.
By her sickbed the madam lay in wait
to coax her into line with chosen words:

"How many lives can anybody claim?
My fresh-blown bud, your spring has just begun!
Someone or other must have grossly erred—
you'll be excused from welcoming our guests!
Now that you've somehow strayed into this home,
well, lock your chamber—wait for the right man!
As long as you're on earth, you own the earth!
You'll find some decent match with a young heir.
Why visit scourge and woe on blameless heads?
You'd lose your life and hurt me too—what for?"

These pleading words were whispered in Kieu's ear—
they sounded with the ring of crystal truth.
Besides, there was the message in her dream:
from Karma no escape—that's Heaven's law.
Why die and leave her debt unpaid for now
to pay with interest in some future life?

She listened, let the words sink in, then said:
"All this has come to pass against my wish.
If your promise is kept, I'll thank my stars.
But will tomorrow's deed match today's word?

I dread to entertain your guests and friends,
to cater to those bees and butterflies!
Better die and stay clean than live in mud!"
  "My daughter, ease your mind," the bawd affirmed.
"I'm not about to humbug you in sport.
If later I renege and force your hand,
there is my judge—the noontide sun above!"
Kieu heard an oath that left no room for doubt—
relieved, she started living once again.
  In Crystal-Blue Pavilion, now her jail,
only the moon and mountains were her friends.
On every side her ranging eyes could see
the downs of gold, the trails of ocher dust.
She dully spent her days in watching clouds,
her nights in staring at the lamp—her soul
half sick for love, half sorrowed by the view.
She thought of him who once, under the moon,
had shared with her the cup of plighted troth—
now, day by day, he longed for her in vain.
Cast up and stranded on a foreign shore,
when could she ever free her heart of love?
She missed her parents so. These days and nights,
they leaned against their door, awaiting her.
Who now in summer fanned them cool, who now
in winter covered them with warming quilts?
In the home yard, as sun and rain took turns,
the old catalpa must have grown so large
that it would take both arms to go around.
  She sadly watched the harbor in gray dusk—
whose boat was that with fluttering sails, far off?
She sadly watched the river flow to sea—
those flowers adrift and lost, where would they end?
She sadly watched the sweep of wilted grass,

the pale-blue haze where mingled earth and sky.
She sadly watched the wind play with the waves
that roared and rolled about, beneath her seat.

Hemmed in on every side by hills and streams,
the exile cried her anguish in a poem.
Forlorn, she let the beaded curtain down
when she heard a male voice across the wall—
it answered her in verse, with the same rhymes.
He was a man still in his freshest youth,
tricked out from head to foot, cocooned in silk—
he seemed one born and nurtured among books.
She later asked and learned his name: So Khanh.
He had peeked through the blinds to watch her there.
When she looked toward him, he declared his love:
"Ah me, a beauty fit for gods and kings!
By what caprice of chance did she stray here?
She should reign on the moon, above the clouds!
How could so fair a flower have drooped so low?
Within I rage at Heaven, the old fool!
Would she could fathom you, O my true heart!
If she but knew, here is the very man
to free her from her cage—it's mere child's play!"
The outside shutters had closed tight again,
but in Kieu's ears his promise still rang clear.
She thought of him, then she thought of herself.
His pity touched her—she felt less alone.
She had long tarried here—her days dragged by:
when could she ever leave this dreary life?
She took the chance—she wrote, imploring him
to save her from the ocean of her woes.
A piece of paper told her tale at length:
how she had paid a daughter's pious debt
and how they had misled her to this den.

At morning, as dawn burned away the haze,
she had her missive smuggled to the man.

The gold-lit sky was blurring in the west
when in response a note from him arrived.
She opened it at once. It was quite brief:
two characters, *hsi yüeh*,[3] in clean-cut strokes.
She tried to penetrate their hidden sense:
"Flee on the twenty-first, hour of the dog?"

Through the dark woods some birds were straggling home.
Over camellias peeped half of the moon.
Leaves stirred their shadows on the Eastern wall—
So Khanh pushed up the window and crept in.
Abashed, Kieu rallied heart to welcome him.
Upon her knees, she whispered an appeal:
"This humble girl, once led astray from home,
is now a captive in the house of mirth.
If from this living death you'll rescue me,
I will knot grass,[4] I will fetch the jade rings—[5]
forever shall I be your grateful slave!"

He listened, then he muttered with a nod:
"I am indeed the one to rescue you!
Since you trust me and turn to me for help,
of course I'll pull you from your sea of woes!"

"I'll put myself in your kind hands," she said.
"Please fix upon whatever plan will work."
He told her: "I have horses fleet as wind—
and at my call a fellow made of brawn.
Let's grasp our chance to slip away from here.
Of all the schemes on earth, it's best to flee!
And if something or other turns amiss,
I shall be there to shelter you from harm!"

Her suspicion was quickened by his words,
but she had gone too far to draw back now.

She shut her eyes and headlong flung herself
to see whither the world would sweep her off.

   Together they stole down the stairs and fled—
each on a horse, the girl behind the man.
The water-clock was dripping, dripping low—
the autumn night was waning, watch by watch.
Wind blasts shook trees and scattered leaves about.
The woods and hills had swallowed up the moon.
Grass wanly gleamed with dew along the trail.
As step by step Kieu went, she yearned for home.

   In throaty chorus cocks were crowing dawn
when from the rear Kieu heard a hue and cry.
Her heart began to pound inside her breast,
for her rescuer had turned rein and fled.
She knew not what to do, left all alone
to jolt her way in terror through the woods.

   O Creator, how could you have the heart
to crumple up and trample on a rose?
A band encircled her—she had no claws
to burrow an escape, no wings to fly.
The bawd arrived in haste upon the scene
and brutally dragged home the fugitive.
In a cold rage, without further ado,
she beat the flower, she flailed the willow tree.
Can one of flesh and blood endure the pain
when they tear at the flesh and spill the blood?

   Kieu sued for pity as she owned her guilt,
bowing her mangled back and bloodied head:
"I'm nothing but a weak and humble girl
who left her distant home to founder here.
In your two hands you hold my life and death.
Brought to this pass, I can no longer care—
my very fate now counts no more with me.
But would you lose the money you laid out?

An eel ought not to mind soiling its head—⁶
hereafter, I'll discard my maiden shame."

The bawd seized on Kieu's word—in black and white,
she forced a pledge someone should guarantee.
Among the inmates was a girl, Ma Kieu—
moved to pity, she offered to stand bond.
Still wroth, the bawd kept breathing fire and hell
for a long time before she would relent.

They carried Kieu inside to nurse her wounds.
Ma Kieu spoke out her mind and counseled her:
"You fell a willing victim to a cad!
Who under heaven doesn't know So Khanh?
A faithless rake who preys on the Green House!
His single hand has nipped many a rose.
His was the feint of the swordsman in flight.⁷
Both pimp and bawd connived in your escape—
as thick as thieves and up to their old ploy.
Some thirty liang had passed from her to him—
if not, would he have acted out that farce?
Now that the joke is done, he'll turn about—
watch what you say or he might harm your life!"
"He swore to me a solemn oath!" cried Kieu.
"How can a person weave such deep deceit?"

While Kieu still mourned her past and future woes,
out of nowhere the brazenface showed up.
So Khanh harangued for all the world to hear:
"It's rumored that a wench lives in this house
who claims I tempted her and led her wrong!
Let her look in my face and name my name!"
"Let's drop the matter if you wish," said Kieu.
"If somehow you deny we ever met,
then I agree we never met, that's all!"

Her words incensed him—screaming epithets,
he came at her with fists ready to strike.

"O Heaven," she exclaimed, "you do know who
devised my ruin, playing false with love!
He meant to push me down a dreadful pit!
In the same breath he swore and he forswore!
But here it is, the note in his own hand—
I met him face to face and no one else!"

Her forthright words were heard by one and all.
They cursed him, his foul deed, his heartless trick.
The lover's perfidy was plain as day—
crestfallen, he maneuvered a retreat.

Alone in her own room, Kieu sobbed and wept.
In black despair, she brooded on her lot.
O shame! A flower, snow-pure and silver-white,
to be the sport of every whirl of dust!
But life is transient, be it grief or joy.
Are fair women not destined to pass on?
In earlier lives she had committed sins:
now in this life she'd pay for her past deeds.
Her innocence was lost—a broken vase!
With her body she'd expiate her guilt.

The mirror of the moon was shining bright—
the bawd now sat by Kieu to lecture her:
"The trade of love does take much toil and care,
and we who ply the trade must know its tricks!"
"I shall submit to winds and rains," sighed Kieu.
"Since I must give myself, so be it then!"

"If girls were all alike," the bawd went on,
"why would the men come here and spend their gold?
There are more things to love than meet the eye,
and ways to cope with men by day or dark.
My daughter, here they are—know them by rote.
Learn seven steps to snare and capture men.

Learn all eight ways to pleasure them in bed.
Play love with them till you've played them all out—
till heads will swim, till hearts of stone will spin!
Now flirt with eyes, now feign anger with brows.
Now sing the moon, now disport among flowers.
There you have it, this house's stock in trade!
Possess it all—you'll have mastered your art!"

    From end to end Kieu listened to the talk
with nervous frown and pallor on her face.
She felt ashamed to bend a maiden ear
to such vile things. How queerly runs the world!
She had been born and raised in a good home
only to go and learn these odd new skills.
And soon her face would grow inured to shame.
No human life could sink below her state!
Alas, what could she do, alone and lost,
when wicked strangers held her in their grip?

    Down came her curtains in the Green Pavilion.
Her price was high—she was the more desired.
The bees and butterflies swarmed round the rose
for long rollicking nights, for months of spree.
Birds thronged the branch, winds stirred the leaves.[8] She'd
                                        speed
Sung Yü at dawn, wait for Ch'ang-ch'ing at dusk.[9]
In the still night, when wine fumes had cleared off,
she would wake up and curse her destiny.
Brocade and silk had once protected her—
now torn to shreds, the rose lay on the road.
Poor calloused face, the toy of winds and dews!
Poor body frayed by bees and butterflies!
O let them rage and storm upon her flesh!
Did she herself know what they all called love?

    The months and seasons rolled. She would embrace

a summer breeze or nestle with spring flowers,
watch winter snow half bury window shades
or bask in moonbeams on an autumn night.
But her own gloom would tinge each sight and scene—
when you are sad, is nature ever gay?
She would write verse or paint, would pluck the lute
beneath the moon or play chess in a bower:
all joys she had to feign and did not feel.
Who knew her heart? With whom could she converse?
Wind in bamboos, rain on plum trees—no charm
could captivate her eyes. A hundred thoughts
all harried and beset a single soul.

  Things of the past, remembered, rent her heart—
a tangled skein of cares, a nest of wounds.
Oh how she missed the two whom she still owed
the Nine Great Debts![10] Day by day they decline
like setting sun on the mulberry tops.
Beyond the far-flung hills and deep-sunk streams,
how could they guess what she had now become?
They had two children left, but still so young!
Without her there, who now could tend their needs?
She still recalled her vow of deathless troth—
so far away, did he know of her plight?
He had come home to ask for her he loved—
but she, another Willow on Chang Terrace,[11]
had been snatched off to pass from hand to hand!
She hoped his love could somehow be repaid.
Had he and sister Van united yet?
Had they grafted the flower upon the bough?
  All her emotions tangled like sleave silk.
Awake in the long night, she dreamed of home.
Beside her window, lone and desolate,
she peered afar into dusk after dusk.
Time fled on moon-hare's feet and sun-crow's wings.[12]

Kieu mourned all women in the League of Sorrow.
Fate grants them beauty as a seeming gift
and makes them pay for it in coin of grief.
It dooms them to a life of wind and dust—
the sneers it hurls at them will not soon cease.

And now from far away arrived a man—
Ky Tam of the Thuc clan, a scholar's son.
From Hsi District, Ch'ang County, he and his sire
had come to open up a trading shop.
He had heard praise of Kieu, beauty's own queen—
he called on her, presenting his red card.
   Behind the tasseled drapes he faced the flower;
his fancy feasted on her every charm:
on its young stem the camellia in bloom
would glow still brighter with each fresh spring shower!
Man and girl, girl and man—one fevered flesh:
on a spring night, how could they quell their blood?
When two kindred souls meet, one single tie
will bind them both in one unslipping knot.
By day and dark, the pair together cleaved—
what had begun as lust soon turned to love.
   For them a stroke of timely luck conspired:
the father left upon a journey home.

The young man's senses ever more bewitched,
he'd visit her again and then again.
On wind-swept balconies, in moon-washed yards,
they'd pour and drink a wine fit for the gods
or improvise linked verse in magic lines.
With morning incense, tea in afternoons,
they would deploy their men to fight at chess
or touch the silken strings to play duets.
One swirling round of pleasures caught them both—
each came to know the other's moods and whims:
to each the other grew more deeply tuned.
    A woman's charms, O wondrous tidal waves—
they sweep away a fortress like a toy!
Young Thuc who squandered money with both hands
could spend his all on a seductive smile.
The bawd sleeked up Kieu's hair and decked her face.
The smell of coins excites a miser's blood.
    The cuckoos cried for summer 'neath the moon.
Above the wall, pomegranate trees displayed
their fiery blooms. Now in her leisure hour,
Kieu dropped the curtain for an orchid bath.
Such pure-white ivory, such unblemished jade—
her body stood as Heaven's masterwork!
He gazed and gazed—transported with delight,
he wrote a T'ang poem[1] to sing his love.
    "I'm touched and glad to know your heart," she said.
"Each word is pearl or jade, each line brocade!
However trifling is my knack for verse,
I ought to answer you in the same rhymes.
But, homesick, I'm in a contrary mood.
My absent mind still dwells with my dear kin—
they live somewhere beneath those golden clouds.
Please pardon me for failing you today."
    He was surprised: "What a strange way to talk!

Or are you not this woman's rightful child?"
A somber cast bedimmed her limpid eyes—
the sense of her own doom swept over her:
"I'm just a flower that's fallen from its branch—
and you're the butterfly that flits and flirts!
Somewhere, no doubt, you keep your wedded wife.
Why waste our brief few days on futile chat?"
  He answered: "Ever since I met you, love,
I've nourished the fond hope of wedding you.
But if we are to live as lifelong mates,
I must inquire and learn about your past."
  "I humbly thank you for the thought," said Kieu.
"But I fear snags—on both your side and mine.
If you have lingered in the Bower of Joy,
you love this flower for its fresh hue alone.
Someday, its bloom will fade, its scent will fail:
will you still care for me or change your heart?
What's more, within the threshold of your home,
a mistress is already holding sway.
You and your wife have weathered out these years:
a concubine will come between you two.
A drifting cloud, a duckweed—who am I
to steal your love away from your sworn spouse?
Should turmoil wreck your home because of me,
who'll pay for such mishap in afterlife?
If at the helm you steer with a firm hand,
you may take sides with me once and again.
But if the lady lords it over you,
I'll fall a prey to her, your lioness!
Under her claws I'll have to crouch and cringe.
Her vinegar will burn worse than hell's fire!
There is your father, too, above your wife:
will he bestow on me a little love?
For if he spurns the rose picked off a wall,

I'll leave this hell only to be sent back.
I'll learn to live with yet more dirt and filth.
But what I'm mindful of is your good name.
If you love me in truth, protect our love.
Remove all risks and I shall do your will."
    "Oh what a guarded tongue you speak!" cried Thuc.
"Are they two strangers still, your heart and mine?
Be not deterred by perils far remote—
rely on me to straighten it all out.
Once we are married, none shall sever us.
To keep you I shall run through sword and fire!"
    They then exchanged the secrets of their souls.
They pledged their faith in sight of sea and hills.
The night was all too short for love refrains:
the moon had dived behind the western heights.

    Young Thuc pretended they were going out
to breathe the cool at some bamboo retreat—
and he hid Kieu away in his own home.
To gain his end, he waged both war and peace.
He bade friends woo the law and court the bawd,
then he confronted her with his demand:
outwitted, she gave up and came to terms.
He paid the ransom into her own hands.
For Kieu's release she signed a document:
it was submitted to the powers on high.
Once he had satisfied both laws and men,
Kieu soon escaped the circle of her woe.

    Beneath one roof they lived as man and wife,
daily their love growing more deep and true.
Like fire and incense mutual passion burned—
her jade-and-lotus beauty gleamed and shone.

    Together they lived thus for half a year.
Now, in the yard, the *wu-t'ung*[2] tree flashed gold.
Along the hedge, white buds of mums peeped out.

79

The father, one fine day, came riding back.
    When he found Kieu, he flew into a rage.
For his son's sake, he'd split the pair apart—
straightway, his ruthless sentence was pronounced:
back to the Green Pavilion she must go.
    The father's verdict was distinct and clear.
Yet, making bold, the son entreated him:
"I know I'm guilty of a heinous crime.
Thus I deserve your anger—even death.
But my fingers have dipped in indigo:[3]
what foolishly I did, I can't undo.
Had I and she been wed for just one day,
could I still have the heart to hold my lute
and then, without a qualm, rip off its strings?
If you will not forgive and grant us grace,
I'd sooner risk my life than play her false!"
    Nothing availed against such stubborn will—
old Thuc lost patience and invoked the law.
Over a tranquil earth the waves now surged.
A warrant called the lovers to the yamen.
Behind a bailiff they fell into step,
then in the hall they knelt down side by side.
    Raising their eyes, they saw an iron mask,
the face of the law. Like thunder roared the judge:
"Young wastrel! You have had your foolish fling!
That hussy, there, is nothing but a cheat!
A castoff rose with all its scent gone stale,
she's worn powder and paint to dupe the louts.
From the complainant's bill I must conclude
neither of you is free to wed again.
I will uphold the law and judge the case.
You can elect to take one of two paths—
either I will proceed and mete out pain,
or back to the whorehouse shall go the whore!"

"Once and for all my mind's made up!" Kieu cried.
"The spider's web shall not catch me again!
Tainted or pure, I want to live my life!
Let the law wreak its wrath on this young head!"
    "The law be carried out!" shouted the judge.
A peony in shackles, cuffs, and cangue!
She bowed and dared not cry her innocence.
Her cheeks were stained with tears, her brows knit tight.
She lay there in the dust—a mirror smudged,
a branch of apricot all shriveled up.
    O pity Thuc the son! How sad his plight!
He watched her from far off, his entrails torn.
"Because of me she suffers so!" he moaned.
"Would I had listened to her warning voice!
My shallow, simple mind could not think deep
and see I'd cost her all this pain and shame!"
    The judge had overheard young Thuc's lament—
intrigued and touched, he further queried him.
The lover sobbed his story out forthwith.
He told how he had wooed and won the girl:
"She gauged all that might happen, soon or late—
she knew full well that she could come to grief.
It was my fault! I took it on myself
and led an innocent into this plight!"
    The judge felt pity when he heard these words.
He smoothed his brow and thought of some way out.
He told young Thuc: "If what you say is true,
this whore knows right from wrong, in spite of all!"
"Though lowly born and bred," answered young Thuc,
"she's learned to wield the brush and scribble verse."
"A rhymester, too? That's splendid!" laughed the judge.
"Tell her to write a poem—on the cangue!
Let her give me a sample of her skill!"
The girl complied—she raised the brush and wrote:

her verse soon lay before him on the desk.
   "It outshines," cried the judge, "the best of T'ang!
All the world's gold can't buy her charms and gifts!
The man of parts and fair woman have met!
Could Chou and Ch'en[4] have bred a finer pair?
Let's put an end to all this storm and strife.
Why sow discord and break a love duet?
When an offense is tried before the court,
inside the forms of justice mercy dwells.
Let your son's wife become your daughter, too.
Abandon anger, let the case be dropped!"
   A wedding was decreed to tie the knot.
A wind-buoyed sedan-chair bore off the bride
as torches flared against a starry sky.
A band of piping flutes and throbbing drums
led bride and groom to their connubial niche.
Old Thuc admired her virtues and her gifts—
from him no more harsh words or stormy scenes.
Lilies and orchids now perfumed the house
as bitter grief made way for sweeter love.
   Time flew amid delights of wine and chess:
peach pink had waned and lotus green had waxed.
Alone with Thuc in their abode one night,
Kieu's heart misgave her—she spoke of their love:
   "Since this frail girl found her support in you,
the wild geese have returned—a year has passed,
Yet it has brought no tidings from your home.
With the new bride, you've cooled toward the old wife.
I do believe there's ground for some concern—
who could have shielded us from prattling mouths?
If talk and rumor I have heard are true,
your lady speaks and acts with frigid poise.
I hold in dread all such uncommon souls.
How can one ever plumb such pits and depths?

We've lived together for these whole twelve months—
this fact cannot have failed to reach her ears.
Yet, all this while, no sign or sound of her!
Behind her silence I suspect some plot.
I beg you to make haste and go back home.
You'll please her and you'll learn where we all stand.
But to keep up this game of hide-and-seek
and put off telling her—it will not do!"

Young Thuc half heeded Kieu's well-pondered words
and braced himself to think of going home.
Next day, he asked his father for advice—
the old man, too, urged him to make the trip.

To bid adieu and share the stirrup cup,
they left their alcove for the horse-relay.
Ch'in River was a ribbon of pure blue
with willows on the shores waving good-bye.
They sighed and groaned and held each other's hands.
As parting words would die within their throats,
the parting cup would stop short of their lips.

"The hills and streams will sunder us," she said.
"To keep me, though, you need your wife's accord.
The careless glance glides past a crimson scarf,
but the fixed gaze will see a needle's eye.
You want to hide our love? You may as well
blindfold yourself and try to catch a bird!
I'm now your concubine, in fact and law:
when you get there, establish that at once.
Should she, displeased, object and raise a storm,
tell her I know my place and honor hers.
Far better thus than try to cover up
and only brew more mischief afterwards.
If you love me, remember what I say.
A year is a long time, but it will pass.
To mourn this day, let's drain the parting cup.

The cup of joy we'll drink a year from now."
  He climbed his horse, she let go of his gown.
The maple-woods were dyed with autumn shades.
He rode off in a cloud of ocher dust
and vanished into the mulberry groves.
She walked back home to face the night alone,
and by himself he fared the distant way.
Who split their moon? Half stayed upon her pillow,
half followed him along his journey's road.

  Why tell all that the wayfarer went through?
Let's talk about the mistress of his hearth.
She came from an exalted breed: the Hoan clan.
Her father held a post of the first rank—
Minister of the Civil Office Board.
To the wide world she was known as Miss Hoan.
Wafted on winds of chance, the two had met
and linked their destinies for many days.
Though in all things she was above reproach,
few could match her in catching one at fault.

  His garden boasted now a new-blown rose—
so she had heard from every mouth but his.
The fire of wrath kept smoldering in her breast
against the knave whose fickle heart had roamed:
  "If only he had told me the whole truth,
I might have favored her with my good grace.
It would have been uncouth to lose my calm
and gain the stigma of a jealous shrew.
But he thought fit to play his boyish prank
and hide his open secret, who knows why!
He must have fancied distance made it safe
to keep things back from me—well, we shall see!
I entertain no worry on this head.
The ant's inside the cup—where could it crawl?[5]

I shall make them abhor each other's sight!
Her I shall crush and trample underfoot!
In his false face I shall rub sweet revenge!
The villain thinks he'll scuttle this old boat,
but he shall know of what mettle I'm made!"

    She locked her anger up inside her heart
and let the breezy tales blow past her ears.
One day, two louts came bringing a report
and hoped to earn fair wages for their pains.
The lady in high dudgeon thundered forth:
"I loathe those malaperts who'd spin a yarn!
My husband's not a common, vulgar churl!
Mouths with less truth than froth have spat this lie!"
She bade her lackeys give them their deserts,
slapping their mouths and knocking out their teeth.
An awestruck hush now settled on her house—
nobody risked another single peep.
In her red chamber, day and night, she'd spend
her vacant hours—composed, she'd talk and laugh
as though nothing at all were out of joint.

    Still, in her bosom, night and day she seethed.
Then he came home, alighting from his horse.
Both uttered cries of joy and words of love.
Their ardor blazed again, or so it seemed.
How many cups they drank to his return!
But Heaven knew what simmered in their hearts!

    He had come home to sound his wife's intents
and, bit by bit, unveil the truth to her.
Yet as she talked or laughed, sober or gay,
she never once would hint at the affair.
"I've kept my mouth shut tight so far," he thought.
"Why squeal when nobody is sticking me?"
He wavered in a shilly-shally pause,
afraid to pull a vine and shake the woods.

At times, while jokes were bandied back and forth,
the lady would emit some vague remark:
"True love sorts jade from stone and gold from brass.
Our union rests upon implicit trust.
Praise be to all those tongues which spin long yarns—
they peddled such tall tales of your amours!
Had reason failed me, I would have befouled
my mind with scandal and been laughed to scorn!"
    And as she put it in a blithesome tone,
he played along to parry her sharp thrusts.
In dalliance they idled time away,
blending their shadows far into the night
and snuggling cheek to cheek beneath the moon.

    A homely diet of fish grass and tench[6]
soon palled his appetite. Now into wells
some *wu-t'ung* trees began to drop gold leaves.
His soul remembered scenes of streams and lakes—
beyond one pass, sporting with wind and moon,
he had for many seasons loved and lived.
Before he ventured to let out one breath,
she knew his mind. She granted him his wish:
"You've been away from Father for a year.
You should plan soon to go back to Lin-tzu
and visit him as it behooves a son."
    Her words unknit a knot within his breast!
His horse flew him across strange hills and streams.
The sparkling waters mirrored a clear sky,
ramparts wreathed with blue smoke, peaks splashed with sun.
    The moment he had cracked his whip and left,
she too boarded a coach. Back with her kin,
she gave a full account—chapter and verse—
of how he had played truant from her bed.
    "As runs the proverb, to my mind," she said,

"a jealous tantrum's like an itchy mange;
it shames the man—it earns the wife no praise.
So I kept mum and looked the other way,
but I already had my plan worked out.
By land, it takes a month to reach Lin-tzu—
by sea, though, one will get there soon enough.
I've picked some trusted lads to man a boat,
go there and bring her back, with feet in chains.
Then I shall persecute her till she swoons!
I shall torment her for the world to see!
I shall discharge my spleen upon them both
and make of them a mockery for all time!"

  Her mother gave approval to this scheme,
allowed her a free hand and all the means.
They had a boat rigged up with sails and yards.
Two lackeys, Hound and Hawk, recruited thugs.
After the crew was told what it should do,
before the wind the boat made straight for Chi.

  Kieu was now left with her shadow alone.
Mixed threads of gloom ran crisscross in her soul.
Her parents' lives were sinking like sun rays
that skim mulberry tops before night falls.
Had they warm clothes? Did they eat well or ill?
The hair she once had clipped to pledge her love
now reached her shoulders, having grown again—
but what had happened to her sacred oath?
Now ivy-like she twined herself to Thuc:
would Heaven look with favor on their match?
Why had so many wrongs befallen her?
Should she resign herself to loveless nights
and mateless live like Ch'ang-o[7] in her hall?
  An autumn night with breeze kissing the drapes,
with sickle-moon and three stars in mid-sky . . .

To burn incense Kieu went to Heaven's shrine.
She was pouring her soul into her prayer
when from the shrubs a wicked band sprang out
and screamed like devils spewed by very hell.
  The yard was all agleam with their drawn swords.
Before she learned the cause of this ado,
they sprayed on her a drug that drowsed her eyes
and sped her spirit to some worldproof realm.
They carried her and placed her on a horse,
then set to flames Thuc's study and her room.
Beside the river they came on a corpse—
they picked it up and dumped it in the house
where, found, it would be taken to be Kieu.
  The servants, frightened out of wit and sense,
had fled to hide in thickets and in groves.
Old Thuc, who lived a little way from there,
saw fire shoot up and spread—a fearful sight.
He led his men and hurried to the spot
to quench the roaring blaze and search for Kieu.
As the wind rose, so higher rose the flames.
The servants looked and looked—of Kieu no trace.
Wild-eyed and frenzied, they scuttled about
and peered at random into wells and shrubs.
At last they fought their way into her room:
there lay a heap of embers and charred bones.
Meaning no harm, suspecting no foul play,
they took it to be Kieu and no one else.
  Old Thuc broke into sobs and tears—he mourned
the virtuous mate his absent son had lost.
He had the ashes gathered and brought home,
then shrouded, coffined, and consigned to earth.
All needful rites for Kieu had been performed
when overland young Thuc at length came back.
  He stepped into their chamber—there he found

a pile of cinders left in rain and sun,
and four bare walls. He ran to his sire's house
to find her altar in the middle room.

   Alas, who could lend voice to his despair?
Grief bit his heart and sorrow burned his soul.
He rolled upon the ground, he wept and moaned:
"A guiltless girl had to die such a death!
I was so sure we two would meet again!
How could I know we'd said farewell for good?"
The more he thought of her, the more it hurt.
Who ever could benumb and stanch his pain?

   He learned that near those parts a shaman lived
who summoned spirits, knowing the Dark Realm.
On the Three Isles[8] or down by the Nine Springs,
he'd trace the dwelling of departed souls.
Thuc sent rich gifts to him, with a request:
"Please find my sweetheart and learn how she is!"
   Before Kieu's altar down the shaman knelt.
The votive incense sticks had not burned out
when he revived from his death trance and said:
"I could not see her face, but I did learn
that a Karma of woe still weighs her down.
With debts unpaid, how could she die as yet?
Her star does show she's now in great distress.
But you must wait a year for news of her.
And when you both are face to face again,
how strange, you will avoid each other's eyes!"
   When Thuc had heard so weird a prophecy,
dared he believe it? She was dead and gone!
No hocus-pocus was to alter that—
where in this world of dust could she be found?
He mourned his flower and wailed their joys of spring—
how often does one meet a nymph on earth?

                    * * *

He thought the fallen flower had gone downstream—
he knew not she had found her hell on earth
Once they had brought their evil scheme to pass,
the ruffians took the girl aboard their boat.
And then, all sails unfurled and halyards tensed,
it raced the waves again, homebound for Hsi.

Once landed, straight to the palace they went,
and there they turned Kieu over for a fee.
They carried her to the bondmaids' back room
and put her down, still in a heavy drowse.
When she awakened from a happy dream,
her home had vanished! What mansion was this?

Half conscious, half asleep, she fumbled still
when a loud call came from the audience room.
A maid went down at once to bring her there.
Kieu followed her in mortal fear and dread.

Her eyes glanced up and saw a stately hall
inscribed on high: "Heaven's Chief Minister."
Bright candles burned on all sides, in broad day—
upon a couch a lady sat enthroned.
She questioned Kieu, searching out branch and root.
The girl hid nothing—she told all she knew.

A storm of wrath descended on her head:
"You are one of those trollops past all shame!
To me you don't look like an honest girl,
but some runaway wife or escaped slave!
A graveyard cat! A hen prowling the fields!
You hemmed and hawed and could not clear yourself!
I've bought you, soul and body—you're my slave,
and you put on such graces and grand airs!
Where are you girls, you who enforce my law?
Teach her a lesson—deal her thirty strokes!"

"Yes, madam!" cried the bondmaids with one voice.
A hundred tongues could not have saved poor Kieu—

with bamboo rods they showered blows on her.
Whose flesh would not have been all torn to shreds?
Whose heart would not have quaked and burst with fright?
Pity a spray of peach, a sprig of plum,
once more assaulted by the wind and rain.

Now renamed Flower the Slave, Kieu was assigned
to serve the ladies at their beck and call.
With hair unkempt and skin as dull as lead,
she joined the ranks of bondmaids garbed in blue.

An old woman—the palace stewardess—
observing her sweet ways, befriended Kieu.
She gave her lotions that would heal her wounds,
and also words on how to stay alive:

"You take what happens, be it fair or foul.
Still you can save yourself much grief, poor wretch.
Perhaps you must atone for some past sin—
but malice brought you here and no mischance.
Stay on your guard: the walls have eyes and ears.
And when you see your friend—well, look away,
or lightning bolts will strike you from the blue!
For justice can we cry, we flies and ants?"

Teardrops of jade were rolling down Kieu's cheeks—
foreboding seized and held her very soul:
"I've had my ample share of wind and dust—
and now this double load of mud and ash!
Will fortune never let its victims go,
but always hound and set on rosy cheeks?
I sinned in former lives and have to pay—
ah me, a wilted flower, a broken pearl!"

From day to day Kieu served as she was bid,
until Miss Hoan came home to see her kin.
Mother and daughter held a lengthy talk,
then Kieu was summoned. The old lady said:
"My daughter needs a slave to serve her wants.

I'll let you go and be her chambermaid."
    Kieu followed her new mistress and set out,
bound for what other hell she did not know.
There, day and night, on hand with combs and towels,
she stood at beck and call—a model slave.
One evening, as the skies were clear and calm,
Miss Hoan bade Kieu display her skill with lute.
She bowed and tuned the strings—then she struck out
such harmonies as poured wine in the soul.
The young lady seemed moved by Kieu's great gift—
her hard-set face relaxed a line or two.
    Inside a stranger's gate Kieu slaved and lived—
only her shadow knew her grief at night,
by day she locked all sorrow in her heart.
She thought of him she'd married in Lin-tzu—
the two might meet again in afterlife!
All heaven was one white expanse of clouds—
Kieu gazed and asked the sky: Where was her home?

    The days and months whirled round, set on their course.
Caught in her plight, Kieu knew nothing of Thuc.
But in Lin-tzu, since the love-bird was flown,
he lived alone in his now empty room.
He missed her brows, beholding the new moon.
He grieved to sense her fragrance in the air.
Yet when the lotus dies, the asters bud—
time softens pain, and winter turns to spring.
Where could he find the girl he had so loved?
His wound throbbed duller as he bowed to fate.
    Nostalgia wakened longings in his soul
and, sick for home, he made his long way back.
She met him at the gate and gushed with joy.
She asked after his health, about all things.
She ordered curtains lifted for more sun.

To greet the master she bade Kieu appear.
    As Kieu came out, she faltered at each step,
for from a distance she perceived the truth:
"Unless the sun and lights have tricked my eyes,
who else but my own Thuc is sitting there?
I've now discovered what's the awful fact:
beyond all doubt, she's caught me in her snares!
How can a hellish plot be hatched on earth?
And why does mankind harbor such a fiend?
In wedlock he and I were duly joined—
she splits us now into master and slave!
Her face is wreathed in smiles, but deep in there
she manages to kill without a knife!
We stand as far apart as sky and earth.
Alas, what can I say? What can I do?"
    She grew distracted gazing on his face—
her thoughts and feelings raveled like silk threads.
Too awed to disobey, she hung her head
and threw herself face down upon the floor.
The husband was dismayed, at his wits' end:
"Woe's me! But that's my Kieu in my own house!
What cause or reason brought her to this pass?
No doubt somebody's hand has set a trap!"
    Lest he betray himself, he spoke no words,
but still he failed to hold his sobs and tears.
His wife transfixed him with a stare and said:
"You just came home—what could have jarred your nerves?"
"I just removed my mourning," he replied.
"I think of my late mother and still grieve!"
She sang his praises: "What a loving son!
But let's shake off your journey's dust—let's drink
and douse the ennui of an autumn night!"
    Husband and wife exchanged many a toast
while Kieu stood by to fetch and fill their cups.

The lady would berate her, finding fault:
she had to kneel and, face upon the floor,
to offer in both hands each round of drinks.
He wildly carried on like one deranged.
After he drank each cup, his tears would flow.
Averting eyes, he'd talk and laugh by fits.
Then acting drunk, he wanted to retire.

"You slave!" the lady snapped. "Beseech the master
to drain his cup, or I shall have you thrashed!"
Grief bruised his vitals, panic struck his soul—
he took the proffered cup and drank its gall.
The lady talked and laughed as though half-drunk.
To crown the evening, she proposed a game.
"This slave's expert in all the arts," she said.
"I'll make her play the lute and feast your ears!"

All shattered and dumbfounded, Kieu obeyed.
She sat before a screen and tuned the lute.
Four strings together seemed to cry and moan
in accents that would break the master's heart.
Both heard the selfsame voice of silk and wood—
yet as the lady smiled, he wept inside.
He could no more restrain his welling tears—
he stooped his head and tried to wipe them off.
Again the mistress shouted at the slave:
"Why play that doleful air and kill our mirth?
Don't you give thought to anything you do?
I'll punish you if the master feels sad!"
He grew more frantic still—to calm the storm,
he wrenched a grin or two from his numb lips.

By water-clock it was now the third watch.
The lady eyed their faces and looked pleased.
She gloried in her soul: "This sweet revenge
offsets all that in silence I have borne!"
But shrunk with shame and choked with rage inside,

he nursed a wound that rankled more and more.
   To share one pillow they regained their niche—
Kieu huddled by her lamp in the long night:
"So now, at last, the mystery is solved!
How weird, that jealous streak which taints her blood!
To split two lovers, she contrived it all—
she'd part and tear us from each other's eyes.
A gulf now lies between master and slave.
No more light chat! No more thoughtful converse!
Our hands are bound by ties as light as pith
that weigh upon us both like chains of lead!
And by the time we will have struggled free,
what will be left to salvage from our love?
Frail woman that I was, I tripped and fell—
how from the raging sea shall I be saved?"
Alone, she brooded deep into the night.
The lamp's oil ebbed and yet her tears still flowed.
   Kieu served them in their mansion, night and day.
And when the mistress saw her tear-stained face,
she queried her. Kieu chose her words and said:
"I sometimes sorrow for my lot in life."
The lady turned to Thuc, requesting him:
"Will you pry loose some facts from her close mouth?"
   The husband felt all torn and rent within.
Neither would he come out and own the truth,
nor could he bear to watch his love's ordeal.
Lest he draw down more trouble on her head,
he ventured, in soft tones, to question her.
Bowing her head, she knelt down on the floor
and wrote in full the story of her woes.
It was at once submitted to Miss Hoan—
she read and seemed to soften just a bit.
She handed it to Thuc, said with a sigh:
"Her gifts demand respect, her plight compassion.

Had fortune favored her with wealth and rank,
she could have graced a palace made of gold.
Instead, she bobs upon a sea of griefs—
blessed with great talent, cursed by destiny!"

    "You state the truth!" Thuc readily agreed.
"She is a woman much ill-used by fate!
But then it's nothing new beneath the sun.
Show mercy—treat her with a gentler hand."
His wife replied: "In what she wrote she begged
to make her home by the Gate of the Void.[9]
So let it be! I'm pleased to grant her wish
and help her break the circle of her woes.
There in our garden is the Kuan-yin[10] shrine
with everblooming lotus and bo tree,[11]
with myriad plants adorning rocks and pools.
Let her go there to tend the shrine and pray."
    The first glimmer of dawn had lit the sky.
They bore five offerings—incense, flowers and such—
and they led Kieu to Buddha's holy home.
There she renounced the world and vowed to live
by the Three Pledges[12] and the Five Commands.[13]
For a cassock she doffed the slave's blue smock,
assuming a nun's name—Purified Source.
To light and keep an everburning flame,
oil was provided and two altar maids,
Spring and Autumn, stood always by her side.
    In this silent retreat, Kieu now lived near
the Purple Grove[14] and far from the Red Dust.[15]
What could she still hope for in human love?
As long as she was spared the shame and grief
of one who sells her charms, she was content.
At Buddha's feet she buried cares and woes.
With her own hand she copied texts by day
and burned incense by night to say her prayer.

O magic drops from Kuan-yin's willow branch![16]
They put out fires of lust in human hearts
and wash away this valley's dust and filth.

   Since Kieu put on the drab colors of Dhyana,[17]
above the autumn garden a full moon
had crossed the zenith time and time again.
Behind barred doors, inside a close-meshed net,
she would feign calmness under watchful eyes—
but by herself, unseen, she would shed tears.
His study and the shrine stood gate to gate—
yet they seemed kept apart by hills and mounts.

   The husband sighed and moaned within his soul.
One day, the wife went off to see her kin.
Chance beckoned him! He slipped out and walked straight
into the garden and met Kieu alone.
He cried his anguish, bursting into sobs,
and teardrops soaked the flap of his blue gown:
"I must confess I have betrayed our troth
and let you singly shoulder all our woes.
Because I reckoned ill, a woman won.
Helpless and sick at heart, I just looked on—
my tongue was tied and could not tell the truth.
Alas, you came to grief by my own fault—
pure jade was smirched, a spring-green youth was lost.
I would have braved all perils and all risks
to stay with you in death, if not in life.
But I could not—I owed my clan an heir.
I clenched my teeth and split our union up.
I broke an oath engraved on stone and bronze.
My shame will live for the next hundred lives!"

   Kieu said: "A cypress skiff that rides the waves
shall float or sink as fortune will dictate.
When I floundered and foundered in the mire,
how could I hope I'd live until this day?

It is my part to play a drop of rain
that falls as chance directs, to the world's glee.
And yet I grieve to think that lute and strings
did come together once. We two did meet
and wed for a few days, if not for life.
Please find some way to free me from this cage.
You'll prove your love and earn my gratitude."
    "That's been my secret wish," young Thuc replied.
"How can one gauge a human heart's abyss?
I fear a storm will break over your head—
it will bring harm on you and grief on me.
Try to escape—flee as far as you can.
That's all there is to our brief common life.
We'll soon be going our diverging ways:
who knows when we shall ever meet again
and take anew the oath we once did swear?
Streams may run dry and rocks may fall to dust,
but I'll keep loving you—for unto death,
the silkworm shall keep spinning its silk thread."
    Together they evoked their happier days.
They talked and talked, undrained of tender words.
Eyes locked, hands clasped, the lovers would not part.
But from afar a bondmaid flashed the sign
to warn them someone was approaching now.
As he swallowed his shame and made to leave,
in walked Miss Hoan brushing the flowers aside.
    All honey and all smiles, she greeted them,
then asked what wind had blown him to this place.
He groped for an excuse and found a lie:
"I went looking for flowers and came this far.
I've stayed to watch her copy sacred texts!"
"Such beautiful brush strokes!" Miss Hoan exclaimed.
"They hold their own with the best of Lan-t'ing![18]
A pity life has buffeted her so!

Her talent's worth a thousand pounds of gold!"
Both drank a Dhyana brew—red plum-wood tea—
then they strolled back to their room lined with books.

Kieu's gloom and dread increased. In a low voice,
she questioned the bondmaid who told her all:
"The mistress had been there for quite some time.
She stood on tiptoe spying half an hour
and saw it all, every last bit and shred!
She heard your every word, learned the whole truth:
all your untold ordeals, all your sore trials,
the master's cries of grief, your own laments . . .
She ordered me to stay there, by her side.
Once her ears had their fill she went upstairs."
    At this a nameless terror froze Kieu's soul:
"I'll never see her like on earth again!
That was real self-control! That was pure sham!
Oh, the mere thought of her can chill my heart!
She has employed such wiles and cunning ways
that Thuc now lies entangled in her snares.
When she caught us together, any wife
would have boiled in her blood and scowled and snarled.
But no, she kept her calm, she dropped no hints!
She greeted us with cheer, she sweetly talked!
An angry face speaks out what the heart feels,
but deep and dark are those who hate and smile.
I must take my own life into my hands.
Hers are a tiger's jaws, a serpent's fangs.
Unless I grow my wings and fly away,
the day shall come when she will nip the flower.
Why should a duckweed mind a rapid stream?
Destined to drift, it drifts no matter where.
But how, alone and lost among strange folk,
will I fight cold and hunger with bare hands?"

Thoughts scurried back and forth, trapped in a maze.
She saw some gold and silver things at hand:
she took a few, hid them inside her dress.
She heard the drumbeats sounding the third watch.
She heaved herself and climbed across the wall,
then westward picked her way in moonset dusk.
A trail of sand ran between wooded downs
to dwindle off and fade far, far ahead.
Roosters crowed at the moon. She walked and walked,
leaving her tracks on the dew-sprinkled bridge.
Deep into night, along a road unknown,
she braved the wind and weather and went on.

V

Now in the east, over mulberry-groves
the sky had just caught fire. Forlorn and lost,
Kieu knew not where to turn and find a home.
Then a short distance off some temple loomed.
She read the sign—"Cloister of Blessed Peace."
She made straight for the gate and shyly knocked.
A nun who heard the knocking let her in.

On seeing Kieu in plain monastic garb,
the prioress—Giac Duyen—took to the girl.
She asked about her life from root to top.
Yet feeling strange, Kieu skirted round the truth:
"This humble nun's a native of Peking.
I've lived by the Three Pledges for some time.
Later, my prioress herself will come.
But I was told to bring you these two gifts.
Will you accept them with her compliments?"

She showed a golden bell, a silver gong.
The nun cast an abstracted glance and said:

"So you came from Hang Thuy, my good old friend?
It worries me to see you go alone.
Why don't you stay with us till she arrives?"
    Kieu made a home of that small cloud-locked shrine.
She lived in peace, feeding on salt and greens.
She'd chant the sutras she had learned by heart.
She'd tend the lamps and censers as of old.
With loving hands she'd tidy the nuns' cells.
Each day, she'd copy Scriptures on palm leaves
or fly the Buddha's banner in the clouds.
She'd light the tapers in the glow of moon
and set the gong a-pealing through dawn's mist.
The abbess found her mind above the norm—
she treated her with kindness and regard,
and Kieu felt more secure in her new home.
    Time passed until it was the end of spring.
The flowers cast shadows carpeting the earth.
The Silvery River flowed across the sky.
No wind, no cloud—a night made for sweet ease.
A woman came to worship at the shrine
and happened to inspect the bell and gong.
"But they look like those at Miss Hoan's!" she cried.
    In good faith Giac Duyen had received the gifts.
Later that night, she queried Kieu again.
Kieu knew she could no longer hide the truth—
from top to bottom she retold her past.
She added: "Now that things have reached this state,
my weal or woe lies squarely in your hands!"
    When she had heard, the nun grew faint with dread.
Between pity and fear she could not choose.
She whispered in Kieu's ear and spoke her heart:
"The Buddha's Gate is open wide to all,
but what disturbs me is the unforeseen.
My heart would break if something struck you here.

Plan far ahead and flee—you'd be unwise
to sit and wait for the full tide to come!"
   There was Dame Bac who lived somewhere about—
a woman always welcome at the shrine:
she always brought some gift, incense or oil.
She was sent for to lend a helping hand.
With thorough cautioning she was enjoined
to hide the fugitive beneath her roof.
   Too glad to find a haven in high winds,
Kieu did not stop to look before she leapt.
She fell in with another pack of thieves:
one school had trained both Dame Tu and Dame Bac!
The girl possessed those charms that make men sigh—
Dame Bac rejoiced at getting such a boon.
Out of thin air she would concoct her tales
and keep poor Kieu on tenterhooks of fear.
Repeating she would turn Kieu out of doors,
she uttered threats to force a man on her:
   "You're all alone, ten thousand miles from home—
and you have earned yourself a spicy name!
Why must I harbor trouble in my house?
Who else but I would dare to shelter you?
At your first chance catch hold of a good man—
or somehow fly to heaven and abscond!
Around these parts no match can be arranged,
nor is there any prospect farther off.
But lucky you! My clan's got just the man!
My nephew, mind! No vagrant in the street!
In T'ai District he owns his house and shop.
The soul of honor! Never breaks his word!
Listen to me and marry him—you must.
Once married, you can move with him to T'ai.
Who'll recognize you there? Free as a bird,
you'll flap your wings and rove the streams and seas!

If you ignore this piece of sound advice,
you'll flout my wish and come to a bad end!"
   Care knit Kieu's brow, gloom overcast her face.
The more she heard, the more it hurt like blows.
Pursued, she'd fled and slipped into a pit.
The cornered quarry vented its despair:
"I'm just a swallow straying from its flock!
Once wounded by a bow, it fears curved boughs.
If I must take a husband as you say,
I'd like to know the man—his face, his heart!
For who can tell what will fall to my lot
if I rush off and marry sight unseen?
Who wants to buy a tiger in a bag?
If someone really, truly cares for me,
then let him pledge to me his faithful love—
let earth and heaven witness his sworn oath!
Then I will follow him across the seas."
   With Kieu's consent secured, the woman left
to notify her clan and ready things.
Their house was cleaned and decked from roof to floor.
They swept the courtyard, set the altar up.
They washed flower vases, burned the incense sticks.
Bac Hanh, the groom, lost no time kneeling down
to swear by all the gods of hearth and home.
Out in the yard, he'd vowed his steadfast love—
inside the curtains now, due rites were held
to tie the Red Silk Tie of married state.
The nuptials done, he put her in a boat
and, with wind in his sail, set off for T'ai.
   As soon as he steered safely into dock,
Bac went ashore and back to his old haunt.
It was one of those shops—an ancient trade—
where bawds and pimps retailed their women's flesh.
They came, appraised the goods, and named a price:

ten times what Kieu had cost, so she was sold.
A sedan-chair was hired to take her 'home'
while Bac was running off with his false face.

    The sedan-chair had barely reached the gate
when from the house a termagant rushed out.
Kieu was escorted in, then asked to kneel
and make obeisances before a shrine.
It was the same old god with hoary brows
in yet another Green Pavilion, yes!
She cast one sidelong look and knew the truth—
but a caged bird can scarcely up and fly!
    "O cursèd Sign of Peach Blossom!"[1] she wept.
"It let me off and now grips me once more—
a cruel game! I'm heartsick of my lot.
Why have talent and irk the jealous gods?
Turbid water was cleansed by alum once:
how often will the mud be stirred again?
Great Potter's Wheel,[2] arch foe of womankind,
you've spun me long enough—why don't you stop?
Since I left home to wander through the world,
all hopes deceived, I've trusted to blind chance.
What sins are visited on this young head?
Why still strike rosy cheeks now half decayed?
If I cannot escape from Heaven's wrath,
I'll brazen out the death of my spring days!"

    Cool breeze, clear moon—Kieu's nights went round and
                               round.
Then from the far frontier a man turned up.
A tiger's beard, a jaw like swallow's beak,
brows thick as silkworms—tough and fierce, his looks.[3]
His shoulders broad, he stood full ten spans tall.
A towering hero on the battlefield,
he overwhelmed his foes with club or fist

and was adept in all the arts of war.
In all the world he knew no law but his—
he was Tu Hai, a native of Yüeh-tung.
He roved on streams and lakes, plying his oar,
with sword and lute upon his shoulders slung.

In town for fun, he wondered at Kieu's fame
and let a woman warp a hero's will.
He brought his calling card to the Green House.
Thus eyes met eyes and heart encountered heart.
"My soul has found its mate!" Tu said to Kieu.
"I do not play at love like giddy fools.
I've heard them rave about your charms and moan
that none of them earned grace in your clear eyes.[4]
But then how often do you see a man
and not a fish in bowl or bird in cage?"

    "You're overpraising me," the girl replied.
"Who am I to disdain this man or that?
It's true I seek the touchstone for the gold.
But oh, where shall I ever find the one
to whom I can entrust my heart and soul?
All come through the front door, leave by the back!
Am I allowed to sift pure gold from dross?"

    "I like the way you put it!" he exclaimed.
"It calls to mind that verse on Prince P'ing-yüan.[5]
Come here and take a good, close look at me:
am I entitled to a bit of trust?"

    "Large is your heart," Kieu said. "One of these days,
Chin-yang[6] may watch you mount the dragon throne.
If you care for this weed, this lowly flower,
please favor me and keep me in your grace."

    Delighted, he approved her with a nod,
then broadly grinned and said: "How many friends
have understood my soul? But your sharp eyes
have seen the hero hidden in the dust!

You spoke one word that proved you've read my thoughts.
If I should conquer myriad pecks of grain
and win a thousand chariots by main force,
I shall still keep you always at my side!"
They found two hearts throbbing in unison—
unbidden, love will come to those it picks.

   Tu thereupon approached a go-between
and paid some hundred liang for Kieu's release.
They built their nest in a quiet retreat:
they laid a bed fashioned of precious woods
and decked their curtains with fairies and gods.
A hero wedded to a heroine—
two phoenix mates soared high on wings of love,
both rode one dragon toward unclouded bliss!

   A year half gone, their love was burning bright—
but now he heard the call of the four winds,
and wanderlust awoke within his breast.
He gazed afar upon the sky and sea,
then grabbed his sword and leapt onto his horse.
   Before he took the road, Kieu begged of him:
"A woman's proper place is near her man.
If you must go, I want to go with you."
"We know each other's hearts, don't we?" he asked.
"And yet you carry on like all the rest!
When I can lead a hundred thousand men,
when all my bugles blare and blast the earth,
when all my flags throw shadows on the roads,
when the wide world at long last knows my face,
then I shall take you home to be my bride!
On the four seas there's nowhere I belong.
If you're to come, you'll only hinder me,
since I can't even tell which way I'll go.
Have patience, wait for me a little while.
I shall be back no later than a year."

This said, he tore himself away and left—
wind-winged, the eagle soared to hunt the skies . . .
    Beside the window where a plum tree bloomed,
with her own shadow Kieu passed endless nights
inside the doors now shut and bolted fast.
No more footprints upon the moss-clad yard.
The weeds ran wild, but the willow grew gaunt.
Her eyes would peer beyond ten thousand miles
to reach the elms and catalpas back there,
and riding clouds her fancy would fly home.
Her heart ached for her parents once again.
Had time allayed their sorrow at their loss?
She had been gone from them for ten long years—
by now, their skin must have grown scales of age,
their heads must be all covered with white frost.
Oh, how she sighed and mourned for her dead love!
In her mind she had snapped the lotus stem,
but its silk fibers still clung to her heart.
If her sister and he had joined their lives,
she must be cuddling children in both arms.
An exile's yearning thoughts of her far home
entwined and interwove with other cares . . .
    After the eagle vanished into space,
Kieu kept her eyes fixed on the edge of sky.
She waited night and day, holding her breath.
Then through the region roared the flames of war.
Vapors of slaughter rose and blurred the air,
as rivers teemed with men who fought like sharks
and roads with killers swathed in coats of mail.
Her friends and neighbors all exhorted her:
"Flee somewhere and remain out of harm's reach!"
But she replied: "I gave Tu Hai my word.
Though I expose my life, I must keep faith."
    Perplexed, she was still wondering what to do

when she saw flags and heard a din outside.
Armor-clad troops had surrounded the house.
"Hail to our Lady!" they set up a cry.
Ten officers, arrayed in two straight lines,
laid down their weapons, doffed their coats of mail,
then knelt and knocked their heads upon the ground.
Now maids-of-honor and attendant dames
came forth to say: "It so pleases our Lord
that we escort you home to be his bride!"
     The phoenix chariot, draped with phoenix veils,
stood ready. Feathers fluttered in the wind
and robes shot sparkles like sun-gilded clouds.
They hoisted flags, beat drums, and off they marched.
A band of pipes and strings led the proud way
and golden sedan-chairs brought up the rear.
Flaunting their badges, heralds rushed ahead.
     Drumbeats resounded through the Southern Court,
convening to Headquarters one and all.
On ramparts banners waved and cannons boomed.
     Lord Tu himself rode out to the camp gate
and welcomed Kieu. He wore turban and sash
with fitting grace—still he was his old self:
swallow's beak jaw and silkworm brows. He cried:
"The fish is back in water—back with you!
Do you remember what you told me once?
To spot a hero took a heroine!
Tell me, have I fulfilled your fondest hopes?"
"I'm just a humble girl," she said, "a vine
lucky enough to grow in the oak's shade.
It's only now we see our dream come true,
but from the first I knew it in my bones!"
Elated, laughing, the lovers locked eyes,
then hand in hand retired to their own tent.
     They gave a feast to treat their valiant troops.

The war drums roared, the battle trumpets brayed.
Triumph was fit reward for hard times past,
and day by day their love bloomed forth afresh.

At camp Kieu settled. In a carefree hour,
she told Tu of those squalid days gone by.
In turn she talked of Wu-hsi and Lin-tzu—
she told how in this place she had been wronged,
how in the other she had been well-loved:
"My life has now laid down its load of woes.
But still I'm bound, in honor, to dispense
reward or punishment as suits the case."
    Lord Tu gave ear to her detailed account,
then like a thunderblast his anger burst.
He mustered his best troops and named their chiefs.
As banners flew, he bade them march at once.
They followed the red flag that showed the way—
one wing rushed to Wu-hsi, one to Lin-tzu.
    Those villains who of old had served Kieu ill
were hunted down and taken back to camp.
A herald was dispatched to take such steps
as would protect Thuc and his clan from harm.
The palace stewardess and the old nun
were bidden to attend as honored guests.
An order of the day put forth the facts:
all were outraged and cried for meet revenge.
    Upon the wicked, Heaven's scourge came down.
They, at one haul, were caught and brought to book.
Wielding broad swords and flourishing long spears,
the guardsmen massed inside the judgment tent;
outside, the soldiers fell into two lines.
All pomp and pageantry in readiness—
the ground was thick with cannons, dark with flags.
    Beneath the tent erected in the midst,

Lord Tu assumed his seat by his fair queen.
No sooner had the drumroll died away
than he called all the captives to the gate.
"Whether they used you ill or well," he said,
"let them receive their wages from your hand!"
"May I borrow your might and power," Kieu asked,
"to pay the proper dues of gratitude?
I'll render good before I take revenge."
"Consult your own sweet will!" Lord Tu replied.

    A swordsman was now sent to fetch young Thuc.
His face dripped sweat of fear like indigo,
and his whole body trembled like a leaf.
"My debt to you weighs a mountain," Kieu said.
"Do you remember me, your Lin-tzu spouse?
Like the Morning and Evening Stars, alas,
we two were split and went our separate ways.
Since it was not your fault, I'd never dream
of overlooking what I owe you, friend.
Brocade, ten bolts; silver, a thousand pounds—
this is a poor return for your good deeds.
Please take this as a token of my thanks.
Your wife, though, is a fiend in woman's guise!
This time she'll find her match at my own hands.
The proverb says, 'Thief and old woman meet!'[7]
Inside the cup the ant shan't crawl for long!
Her deep-laid scheme shall be repaid in kind!"

    Thuc's haggard face was wondrous to behold—
it was perspiring like a shower of rain.
His heart was bursting with both joy and fear—
fear for his wife and joy at seeing Kieu.

    Next came both palace stewardess and nun:
to seats of honor they were promptly led.
Kieu held their hands, then she took off her veil
and showed her face. "My friends, look here!" she cried.

"Remember? Flower the Slave, Purified Source,
and I, your servant, are one and the same!
When my foot slipped and I fell in the pit,
you pitied me, and for my sake you did
more than a hill of gold can now repay.
A thousand liang is meager recompense.
For, to Han Hsin,[8] the washerwoman's heart
was worth much more than all the gold on earth!"
The women, disbelieving what they saw,
stood stupid, torn between awed dread and joy.
Kieu told them: "Stay where you are now, I beg,
and watch how I will settle scores with them!"

Guardsmen were bid to fetch the prisoners—
all proofs of their misdeeds were now perused.
Swords were unsheathed and raised beneath the flags.
The chief culprit came in—her name: Miss Hoan.
Kieu greeted her as soon as she appeared:
"Your Ladyship! You, too, have deigned to come?
One seldom finds a woman of your stamp!
How many in the past could boast your face?
How many now can beat you in sheer gall?
A woman, though, should wield a gentle hand—
the more evil she sows, the more she reaps!"

Miss Hoan's spirit and soul were taking flight.
She knocked her forehead on the earth and cried:
"I'm but a woman with a woman's faults!
And jealousy is human, after all!
Yet please recall that I did let you stay
and copy Scriptures at the Kuan-yin shrine.
When you fled from my house, I let you go.
In my own heart I felt esteem for you,
but what woman would gladly share her man?
I'm sorry I cast thorns before your steps—
may I implore your mercy on my fate?"

Kieu said: "To tell the truth, you have a wit
that few can match! And you know how to talk!
If I spare you, you'll have to thank your luck.
But if I strike, I'll seem petty and mean.
A contrite heart should mitigate your crimes."
She gave an order to release Miss Hoan,
who gratefully fell prostrate on the ground.
   Now a long string of prisoners filed in.
"Heaven above, you saw it all!" cried Kieu.
"Let evil deeds atone for evil deeds!"
Before their judge came Bac Hanh and Dame Bac,
then Hawk and Hound, these followed by So Khanh
and by Dame Tu the bawd and Scholar Ma:
guilty as charged, how could they go scot-free?
The executioner received the word—
he set about fitting each penalty
to such an oath as each had rashly sworn.
Blood flowed in streams while flesh was hacked to bits—
the scene struck terror into every soul.
In heaven all the acts on earth are judged.
He that has wrought must pay—such is the law.
And they who had committed fiendish sins
could cry no quarter, paying with their lives.
The army was assembled on the grounds
to watch justice divine carry the day.
   Kieu's hand had dealt just wages to them all—
Giac Duyen arose to take her leave. Kieu cried:
"Once in a thousand years! Is that the most
the very best of friends can hope to meet?
Duckweed and cloud will meet and drift apart!
A crane that roams the fields, a cloud that haunts
the hills and woods—where are you to be found?"
   "It will not be too long," the nun replied.
"We shall hold hands again within five years.

As I remember, on my pilgrim's way
I ran across a prophetess, Tam Hop.
She forecast you and I would meet this year,
then yet another time five years from now.
Her prophecy has hardly missed the mark!
Now proven true, it shall prove true once more.
For Karma binds us still with many ties—
why should you fear our paths won't cross again?"
"Yes, destiny can be foreseen," Kieu said.
"What the seeress has seen, we too shall see.
Should you find her again upon your road,
ask her to tell my fortune yet to come."
Giac Duyen promised. They traded words of love,
then the nun left and soon passed from Kieu's view.

When Kieu had given gifts and punishments,
like a vast sea the bitter sense of wrongs
ebbed in her heart. She knelt before Lord Tu
to say her thanks: "Weak and frail as a reed,
I never hoped I'd call this day my own.
For me your lightning brought the wicked low
to cast a weighty burden off my soul.
I've etched your favors in my flesh and bones—
my very life could not repay my lord!"

Tu answered: "Have the great men of all times
often met that one friend who knows their heart?
And does a hero live up to his name
who finds a wrong and lets it go unrighted?
Also, I did it for my family!
Why should you stoop and offer me your thanks?
But you still have your parents, and I grieve
to see you live in Yüeh and them in Ch'in!
I shall not rest at ease until the day
when you will be restored to all your clan."
At Tu's command the feasting-boards were spread.

From captains to their men, all gathered round
to celebrate the ending of Kieu's woes.
   From victory to victory Tu swept—
a slit bamboo will split all by itself,
and one slipped tile will topple the whole roof.
His fame like thunder rumbled far and wide.
In his own territory, he held court
and named his ministers for war and peace.
His fiefdom cleft the empire in two halves.
Time after time he stormed across the land
and trampled down five strongholds in the South.
He fought and honed his sword on wind and dust,
turning his back on all who were content
to serve as racks for coats and bags for rice.
At will he ruled the empire's borderland—
there he proclaimed himself a prince, a king.
Under his flag none dared dispute his sway.
For five years, by the sea, he reigned sole lord.
   Now came a great Commander General:
Lord Ho Ton Hien possessed a statesman's craft.
His Majesty himself had seen him off
as field marshal of troops on this campaign—
Ho held the fullest powers to quell revolt.
   He knew Tu Hai would prove a gallant foe,
but that in all his plans Kieu had a voice.
He camped his troops and feigned to seek a truce.
He sent an envoy, loading him with gifts
—jade, gold, silk, and brocade—to coax Tu Hai
to yield. There were rich presents, too, for Kieu:
two maids-of-honor and a thousand pounds
of gold and jade.
               The envoy reached the camp.
Tu was assailed by gnawing doubt. He mused:
"My own two hands have built this realm of mine.

I roam the streams and seas just as I wish.
If I submit, surrender all my power,
and show my shamed, confounded face at court,
what will become of me among them all?
Why let them swaddle me in robes and skirts?
Why play a duke only to cringe and fawn?
Better indeed to rule my own domain!
What can they really do against my might?
At pleasure I storm heaven and stir earth!
I come and go bowing my head to none!"

But faith in people lingered in Kieu's heart.
Soft words and costly presents won her trust.
"A duckweed floating down the stream," she thought,
"I've wandered long enough, suffered enough.
Let's swear allegiance to the Emperor's rule—
we'll travel far on fortune's royal road.
Public and private ends will both be served,
and soon I could make plans to go back home.
With head erect I'll walk before the world—
my parents will take pride in my new state.
I'll have achieved so much for the realm's good
and done my duty by the family.
That's better than to drift hither and yon
like a lost skiff subjected to the waves!"

When they discussed the wisest course to take,
she sought to talk him over to her views:
"The Emperor's munificence," she would say,
"has showered on the world like drenching rain.
His virtues and good works have kept the peace
and placed the empire deeply in his debt.
Since you rose up in arms, the dead men's bones
have piled head-high along the Wayward River.[9]
Why should you leave an ill repute behind?
Have songs and poems ever praised Huang Ch'ao?[10]

Why not accept high post and princely purse?
Are there two paths to success in the world?"
   Her words struck home: he listened and gave ground.
Dropping his plans for war, he sued for peace.
He parleyed with the envoy and made truce:
he pledged himself to disarm and disband.
Under the ramparts covenants were drawn.
All battles ceased. He slackened his defense
and let the flags hang loose, the drums go dead.
Imperial spies who had been watching him
observed how his camp stood inside and out.
Lord Ho conceived a ruse to snatch this chance.
Behind a screen of gifts he placed his troops,
poised to attack when the right time would come.
The flying flag of truce now led the van,
with gifts on view and guns well camouflaged.
   Lord Tu suspected nothing, caught off guard.
To pledge allegiance he strode out of camp,
accoutered in high bonnet and court robe.
Lord Ho now gave his men the secret cue—
flags on all sides unfurled and cannons roared.
The fiercest tiger, taken unawares,
will be entrapped and meet an abject end!
Facing his doom, Tu fought his one last fight
and showed them all a soldier's dauntless heart.
When his brave soul left him to join the gods,
he still stood on his feet amidst his foes,
remaining firm as rock and hard as bronze—
who in the world could shake or move his corpse?
   Imperial troops pursued his routed men.
The murk of death that none on earth could breathe
billowed in angry fumes to choke the skies.
Through moats and battlements now tumbling down,
a rebel guided Kieu to her Lord Tu.

Round him arrows and stones flew thick and fast—
upright, he held his ground beneath the clouds.
    "You lacked in neither wit nor heart!" she cried.
"But you took my advice and came to this!
How can I bear to look you in the face?
Why don't I die with you, right here and now?"
Her pent-up grief gushed forth in floods of tears.
She flung herself head first upon the field.
O strange affinity of two wronged souls!
As she collapsed, he too fell down with her.
    Some officers and men were passing by.
Pitying Kieu, they raised her up again—
gasp after gasp she found her breath and lived.
To Ho's headquarters they delivered her.
The lord addressed her in a friendly voice:
"Defenseless, fragile woman that you are,
you've been war-tossed and suffered grievous blows.
Our gracious sovereign planned this whole campaign
and foreordained its issue. Nonetheless,
you played a role—you talked the traitor round.
Now all is well that has come off so well—
I'll leave you free to choose your own reward!"
    When Kieu heard this, her eyes poured out more tears.
Heaving with sobs, she unburdened her breast:
"A true hero, Lord Tu! At will he roamed,
his own master between the sky and sea.
He trusted me and did what I advised—
that fighter who had never lost a fight
agreed to lay down arms and serve at court!
He hoped to gain the world for him and me—
alas, he came to nothing in a trice!
Through five whole years he'd ruled his own domain—
and then he had to go and like some trash
throw down his life upon the battlefield!

You counsel me to ask for a reward,
but my heart aches to hear you mention it.
All that I've done deserves more blame than praise.
Would I had ended this now useless life!
Please give me for his grave a patch of earth
to lay to rest a man who died a god!"

Moved by Kieu's plea, Lord Ho had Tu's remains
grass-wrapped and buried on the riverbank.

The troops proclaimed their triumph with a feast.
Strings twanged, flutes piped—all reveled and caroused.
They forced Kieu to attend upon Lord Ho—
he got half drunk and made her play the lute.

She played a tune that moaned like wind and rain.
From her five fingertips blood, as it were,
dripped onto the four strings. The gibbon's howl
or the cicada's cry was not so sad.
Ho listened, knitting brows and shedding tears.
He asked: "What are you playing there that sounds
like the world's griefs and woes all rolled in one?"

"This tune's called Cruel Fate, my lord," Kieu said.
"I once composed it in my early youth—
a long time since. But now, of cruel fate
you have a victim right beneath your eyes!"

Her music stirred his heart, and her fair face
entranced his soul. O miracle of love!
With sweet madness it touched an iron mask.
"Your husband's dead, but you're still young," he said.
"Would you let me retie the knot with you?"

"I'm an unworthy woman," answered she.
"And I still mourn the death of him I killed.
A faded petal—what's there left of me?
My heartstrings broke just like Hsiao Lin's lute strings.[11]
You spared my life—I'll count my luck complete

if I see home again before I die."

Flushed with success, Lord Ho had overdrunk,
but in the morning wit and sense came back.
He now recalled he was a state grandee
whom both his betters and the mob observed.
It ill became a lord to toy with love!
How was he to untangle this affair?
He held an early levee as day broke—
of all expedients he adopted one.
His word was law and not to be gainsaid—
Kieu was compelled to wed a tribal chief.

How wayward can you be, O Wedlock God,
at random spinning and tangling your threads!
The bridal palanquin was carried straight
onto the bridegroom's boat for wedding rites.
Curtains came down and nuptial lamps lit up . . .

Willow all withered, peach blossom all seared—
her freshness was all gone, not one spark left.
She would as soon jump into the swift stream
and let the waves and sands entomb her self,
her parents' love and care, her gifts of mind . . .
Mere flotsam sea-borne toward the world's far bounds,
where would she find a grave and rest her bones?
Who had cut them, her silken ties of love?
And who had trapped her in a hateful match?
How could she be debased to such a state?
For her, to live another day on earth
would only serve to waste another day.
When life meant joy no more but only woe,
why should she not die then without regret?
Her body felt a hundred bitter pains—
let her destroy it all and make an end!

The moon had slipped behind the Western hills.

Alone, distraught, she'd walk and sit by turns.
She heard the muffled voice of rising tides.
She asked and learned the river was Ch'ien-t'ang.
Had not that very name rung in her dream?
Here was the finish of her course of grief:
"O Dam Tien, do you know that I am here?
You promised once we two would meet again.
Please wait for me down there and welcome me!"

She found a slip of paper by her lamp
and wrote a farewell poem, to be her will.
Parting the beaded curtain, she looked out:
river and sky wrapped in one shroud of night.
"Lord Tu was kind to me," she mourned within.
"Yet I betrayed him in the country's cause.
I killed my man, then took another man.
How can I live and show my face on earth?
Ah, I shall perish now and end it all!
Unto the waves let me entrust my heart!"

Kieu cast her eyes upon the shoreless stream,
then head first hurled herself into the waves.
The tribal chief rushed up to rescue her.
It was too late—her fair body had sunk.

O curse the frailty of a human reed—
how can it bear beauty and talent too?
She wandered from one sorrow to the next—
what would be left of her, at journey's end?
For fifteen years, how many times her plight
held up a mirror to all womanhood!
None could have fallen to a lower depth,
and yet, who knows? In the workings of fate,
at dead of darkest night the dawn returns.
Must good daughters and sons go through the worst
to merit Heaven's pity for their woes?

* * *

With gourd and luggage-box the nun Giac Duyen
had walked on mountain trails among the clouds.
And then one day she met Tam Hop again.
She asked the prophetess about Kieu's fate:
"Kieu did all that a daughter could have done—
why has she known nothing but pains and woes?"

"Man's fortunes rest with Heaven," said Tam Hop.
"And yet they also spring from his own heart.
Yes, Heaven shapes our lives, but so do we.
When we renounce the world, we harvest joy.
If passion rules, it ties the noose of grief.
She'd got a lavish share of charms and gifts
and thus invited Heaven's spite and wrath.
Then, too, her hand would weave a net of love
in which at pleasure she'd enmesh herself.
Thus when she dwelt in those abodes of peace,
she would not stay, for she could not sit still.
By fiends inspired, by demons led astray,
she blindly darted down the path of woe.
She raced from grief to grief. Along her road,
she twice repaired to the Green House of Mirth,
and twice she donned the blue smock of a slave.
She lived with bristling spears and naked swords.
She ministered to wolves in human clothes.
She hurled herself into the roaring waves
and tempted the fell jaws of monster-fish.
Grief follows passion—that's the constant law.
She'll walk her lonely way, suffering alone.
On earth she'll know all the torments of hell,
and they shan't end until her lifetime ends!"

This warning shook Giac Duyen with fear and dread.
"Then Kieu is doomed!" she cried. "Is there no hope?"
"All is not lost," the prophetess replied.

"Each action, good or ill, weighs in the scale.
When judged for her past sins, Kieu must be charged
with reckless love, but not with wanton lust.
Requiting love for love, she sold herself
and saved her father: Heaven did take note.
She caused one death, but many lives were spared.
She knew right thoughts from wrong, fair deeds from foul.
Whose merits equal her good works, in truth?
Thus they have washed away her sins of yore.
When Heaven bends an ear, man's voice is heard.
She who has purged herself from her past faults
sows future happiness. Mark what I say—
for old times' sake, down the Ch'ien-t'ang you'll float
a raft or skiff and save a human life.
You'll thus redeem a promise you once made.
It falls on us to do what's Heaven-blessed!"
    At these good words the nun's heart skipped with joy.
She slowly trudged her way to the Ch'ien-t'ang
and settled on its shore. She braided thatch
to build her hut: a shelter nestling there
between the emerald waves and golden clouds.
Year in, year out, she hired two fishermen
to stay aboard their boat moored to the bank
and watch a fishnet stretched across the stream.
She prayed with all her soul and grudged no pains.
It came to pass, for Heaven willed it so.
    After Kieu plunged into the silver waves,
she drifted with the current to this spot.
The fishermen hauled her body aboard—
Tam Hop's prophetic words had now come true.
They laid Kieu down, her robe all dripping wet.
Though water-soaked, her skin still gleamed with life.
The nun could tell it was indeed Kieu's face—
but she was still immersed in a deep sleep.

Her soul was wandering through the grove of dreams—
out of the past appeared a friend, Dam Tien.
"I have been waiting here for you," she said.
"More than ten years I've spent within these wilds.
How frail your life! Your virtues, though, how strong!
Fair women have all known a common fate—
but few, so few have had a heart like yours.
High Heaven has observed your constant faith.
You saved your father when you sold yourself.
You spared uncounted lives the curse of war—
your country and your people were well served.
Such hidden merits have now tipped the scale.
Your name's been struck from the Book of the Damned:
you may reclaim them all, your poems of grief.
Abundant blessings shall be yours to reap—
and your old love shall be fulfilled at last!"

Still dreamy, Kieu knew not what to believe
when someone's voice came whispering in her ear:
"Purified Source!" She wakened with a start.
Mists fogged her eyes—she recognized no face.
Dam Tien was nowhere to be found aboard,
but at her side she soon could see Giac Duyen.

Their mutual joy burst forth a hundred ways.
They went ashore and home to the grass hut.
And now, day after day, they shared one roof.
They cooled their faces in the wind and moon
and cleansed their hearts living on salt and greens.
Around them, on all sides, a waste stretched far—
there, nights and mornings, ebbed and surged the tides
between two banks of clouds in front and back.

VI

Here Kieu shook off the dust of her past life,
but how was she to guess that, at this place,
she'd find her ancient love again one day?
   If a full load of griefs had been her lot,
young Kim himself had suffered much the while.
For mourning rites he had made the long trip
and from Liao-yang came home after six months.
   He hurried toward his dear Kingfisher's nest.
He took one startled look—the scene had changed.
The garden was a mass of tares and reeds.
At moonlit windows he could glimpse no face.
The walls, battered by rain, were crumbling down.
He walked around and failed to see a soul.
Only the peach blossoms of yesteryear
were flirting still with the frolic East wind.[1]
Swallows were darting through the vacant rooms.
Grass hid the ground, and moss the tracks of feet.
Beyond the wall, a clump of thorns and shrubs

blocked up the pathway where they once had trod.
A silent chill was brooding over all.
Who could relieve the anguish of his heart?

A neighbor came and had a chat with him.
Kim asked a thing or two, discreetly phrased.
Old Vuong? Had somehow tangled with the law.
And Kieu? Had sold herself to ransom him.
The family had moved a long way off.
As for young Vuong, the mother, and Thuy Van,
they all were struggling with dire want and woe:
they scribed or sewed, living from hand to mouth.

It hit Kim like a firebolt from mid-sky.
Staggered and stunned by all that he had heard,
he asked where those unhappy folk had gone—
he found his way to their new dwelling place.
A tattered hut with thatch roof and mud walls,
reed blinds in rags, bamboo screens full of holes,
a rain-soaked yard with nothing but rank weeds—
the sight dismayed and shocked him all the more.

Still, making bold, he cleared his throat and called.
On hearing him Vuong Quan came out in haste
and led him by the hand into the house.
From their back room the parents too appeared.
They wept and wailed as they retold their woes:
"O son, you know what happened to us all?
Our daughter Kieu is cursed by evil fate!
She broke her word to you, her solemn troth!
Alas, disaster struck the family.
To save her father—yes, she sold herself!
How wrenched and torn she was when she left home!
In tears she told us time and time again—
since she had sworn to you a sacred oath,
she begged her sister Van to take her place
and in some way redeem her pledge to you.

But her own sorrow will forever last!
In this existence she broke faith with you—
she'll take her vows down to the Hall of Shades
and make it up to you when she's reborn!
These were the very words that passed her lips.
We marked them in our souls before she left.
O daughter Kieu, why does fate treat you so?
Your Kim is back with us, but where are you?"

The more they talked of Kieu, the more they grieved.
The more Kim heard them talk, the more he ached.
He writhed in agony, he sorely wept,
his face tear-drowned and sorrow-crazed his mind.
He suffered so he fainted many times,
then yet more bitter tears succeeded faints.

When he saw Kim disconsolate, old Vuong
curbed his own grief and tried to comfort him:
"What's done can't be undone! The planks of wood
already have been nailed into a boat.[2]
She's now committed to her hapless fate
and never could reciprocate your love.
However much you treasure what is past,
must you therefore throw off your precious life?"

They sought all means to give him ease and balm,
but once allayed, his grief would flare again.
Now they brought out the tokens of his troth—
the pair of golden bracelets—and they showed
those keepsakes from the past: incense and lute.
The sight of them rekindled his despair—
it roused his grief and rent his heart once more.
"Because I had to go away," he cried,
"I let her fall and helpless drift downstream!
We two did take and swear our vows of love—
vows firm as bronze and stone, not idle words.
Though we have never shared the marriage bed,

still we are man and wife as we once pledged.
How could I ever cast her from my heart?
Whatever it may cost, however far
I have to go, as long as I draw breath,
I shall not quit until I see her face!"
    He suffered more than all the words could say.
Stifling his sobs, he left and hurried home.
Within his garden he prepared a lodge,
then he went back to fetch Kieu's parents there.
He saw to their well-being day and night
like their own son, in their lost daughter's stead.
    With ink and tears he wrote for news of Kieu.
To find her, he dispatched his men abroad.
How much he gladly spent on hiring help!
How often he resorted to Lin-ch'ing!
He searched one place—she at another stayed.
Where should he look between the sky and sea?
He yearned and pined. Now desperate, he felt
his soul on fire, his heart under the plow.
He wilted deep inside, thirsty for love.
His careworn body wasted day by day.
He languished thus, half alive and half dead.
He wept real tears of blood but let his soul
depart his body for the realm of dreams.
    His parents took alarm—as his health failed,
they feared the worst might happen to their son.
They read the omens and picked out a date:
an early wedding joined young Kim to Van.
A brilliant scholar and a graceful girl
united gifts and charms in their full bloom.
If he found joy in married harmony,
could it displace the old grief from his heart?
He lived with his new wife—a new love grew,
but only to enhance his other love.

Whenever he remembered Kieu's ordeal,
he wept and felt a tightened knot inside.

  In his hushed study he, at times, would burn
their old incense and play on their old lute.
The strings of silk would whisper their sweet moans
as wisps of scentwood fragrance filled the air
and curtains rippled in a gentle breeze.
Then, coming from the threshold—so it seemed—
he heard a sigh, an echo of Kieu's voice,
and caught the fleeting shadow of her skirt.
He had engraved his love on stone and bronze—
he dreamed of her and thought she had returned.

  His nights and days were steeped in dreary gloom
as spring and autumn wheeled and wheeled about.
One year, it chanced that in the Capital
a state examination was decreed.
On the same day, the names of Vuong and Kim
were added to the *Chin-shih*[3] roll of fame.
The Gate of Heaven then swung open wide
to pilgrims on the Highroad of Blue Clouds![4]
The Emperor feted them in his own park
and glory shone upon their native heath.
Young Vuong still kept in mind those days long gone:
he called on Chung to settle a great debt.
He paid it off in full, then took to wife
his daughter and united the two clans.

  Kim briskly trod the Highroad of Blue Clouds,
but still he thought of Kieu and wept for her.
With whom had he exchanged his vows of love?
With whom did he now share his jade and gold?
Poor duckweed lost in the troughs of wild waves—
amidst his wealth, he mourned her wandering life.

  Then he was sent to serve in far Lin-tzu;
with his loved ones he trekked a thousand miles.

In the yamen he passed his leisured days.
Mornings and nights, he heard no mundane noise—
only the cry of cranes, the sound of lutes.

One night, Van dreamed and saw her sister Kieu—
there in Lin-tzu. She wakened and told Kim.
He wondered, caught between mistrust and hope:
"The names Lin-ch'ing and Lin-tzu sound alike—
they well could be mistaken each for each.
Two kindred souls, Kieu and Van met in dream—
who knows, here in Lin-tzu, glad news may come!"

Young Kim now made inquiries right and left.
One of his scribes, old Do, gave this report:
"It all began more than ten years ago.
I knew them all quite well—faces and names . . .
Dame Tu and Scholar Ma went to Peking—
they purchased Kieu and brought her back with them.
In charm and talent she was without peer—
she played the lute, she wrote fine poetry.
To save her virtue she fought with fierce pride—
she tried to kill herself, so they used tricks.
She had to live a life of wind and dust!
Then wedlock ties attached her to young Thuc.
But his first wife laid cruel hands on her
and hauled her to Wu-hsi to nip the flower.
When driven to despair she had to flee,
it was her luck to fall among more thieves!
No sooner caught than she was sold again.
She drifted and she wandered here and there.
But now a hero chanced upon her road.
In wit and valor second to no man,
he shook and awed the heavens with his might.
He led a hundred thousand seasoned troops.
They came in force and occupied Lin-tzu.
Here Kieu cleared off old scores, wiped out the past:

she rendered good for good and ill for ill,
proving herself a lady, just and wise.
She paid her debts and won the world's high praise.
What is the hero's name? I still don't know—
for this you'll have to query Scholar Thuc."

   After he heard the long account by Do,
Kim sent his card to bid Thuc visit him.
He plied his guest with questions about Kieu—
where was her husband now, who was the man?
"It was a time of stress and strife," Thuc said.
"When at his camp, I learned a few details.
The overlord was Hai from the Tu clan.
A hundred battles he had fought and won—
his strength could hold ten thousand foes at bay.
There in T'ai District he encountered Kieu—
her beauty and his genius then conjoined.
For many years he tore about the world.
He thundered, and earth quaked and heaven quailed!
He garrisoned his soldiers in the East.
Since then, all signs and sounds of him are lost."

   Kim heard and knew the story root and branch.
Anxiety and care oppressed his heart.
Alas for a poor leaf flung to the winds—
how could she ever shake the world's dust off?
As the stream flowed, it bore along the flower—
he mourned her wave-tossed life, detached from his.
From all their broken vows he had preserved
a bit of incense there, and here this lute.
He played it, but its soul had fled the strings.
He burned the incense—would it ever bless
their union in this life with fire and scent?
While she was drifting still so far from home,
how could he wallow in soft ease and wealth?
Instead, the seals of office he'd resign—

then he would cross the streams and scale the heights;
then he would roam over the fields of war
and run all risks in quest of his lost love.
But heaven showed no track, the sea no trail—
where could he seek the bird or find the fish?

He pined away in sighs for news of Kieu
as sun and rain in many cycles passed.
Now from the throne, on rainbow-tinted sheets,
an edict came to hand which ordered thus:
Kim was to take an office in Nan-ping,
while Vuong assumed new functions in Fu-yang.
They hastened to secure carriage and horse,
and then together the two families left.
One day, they heard: "The rebels have been crushed!"
The swelling waves in Fu-kien had calmed down,
and in Che-kiang the flames were flickering out.
Learning the news, young Kim entreated Vuong
to help him and inquire about Kieu's fate—
and thus both traveled on to reach Hang-chow.
There they obtained precise and proven facts.
They got the word: "One day, the fight was joined.
Tu, ambushed, fell a hero on the field.
Kieu's noble service earned her no reward—
they forced her to espouse a tribal chief.
She jumped into the river and she drowned—
the Ch'ien-t'ang has become for her a grave!"

Ah, torn asunder not to meet again!
Now all of them stood high in rank and wealth—
she, innocent and pure, had had to die.

Performing rites to call Kieu's soul, they made
a tablet with her name. For her repose,
they set an altar on the riverbank.
The tide cast wave on silver-crested wave—

they gazed and pictured how the rose had dropped.
Their love for her became a sea of grief:
where could they find the errant bird's lost soul?[5]

Wonder of wonders! Something happened then.
It chanced that old Giac Duyen was walking past.
She saw the tablet and made out the name.
Amazed, she asked: "Who are you all, my friends?
Are you perchance some kith or kin of hers?
But she's alive! Why all these mourning rites?"

They heard the news and nearly fell with shock.
All pressed around the nun to let her know
who each one was and question her again:
"Her husband's here, her parents over there,
and there her sister, brother, and his wife!
We thought we knew for certain she was dead—
but now you give us this most wondrous news!"

"Karma drew us together," said the nun,
"first in Lin-tzu, and next on the Ch'ien-t'ang.
When she would end her life in the stream there,
I stood at hand and brought her safe to shore.
We've taken shelter by the Wisdom Gate,
in our grass cloister, a short walk from here.
And at the Buddha's feet, our days of peace
pass one by one. But still, she misses home."

On hearing the good news, their faces beamed.
What bliss in heaven could exceed their joy?
Since that dark day when the leaf left the grove,
they'd searched through all the streams, scanned all the
                                        clouds.
The flower had fallen and its scent had fled—
that seemed so clear. They might see Kieu again
in some world yet to come, but not in this—
for they and she had split like day and night.
Now, back from the Nine Springs, she walked on earth!

They knelt and bowed their thanks to the old nun,
then in a group they followed on her heels.
They cleared and cut their way through rush and reed,
their loving hearts half doubting still her word.
By twists and turns they edged along the shore,
then all emerged from the wild growth of grass
to reach the courtyard of the Buddha's shrine.
In a loud voice the nun now called to Kieu,
and from an inner room she hurried out.

She glanced and saw her folk—they all were there.
Father was still quite strong, mother quite spry.
Both sister Van and brother Quan grown up.
And standing to one side was Kim, her love.
Where was she now? And was this moment real?
Was she dreaming awake, with open eyes?
Tear-pearls dropped one by one and damped her robe;
her heart was filled with joy and grief alike.

She cast herself upon her mother's knees
and, weeping, told of all she had gone through:
"Since I set out to rove a hostile world
—a duckweed cut adrift, the toy of waves—
fifteen long years have passed. I never hoped
to live, surmounting mud and tide, and now
to reunite with all of you on earth!"

The parents held her hands, gazed at her face:
her looks had little changed since she left home.
But still, the flower and moon of libertines
had been lashed through the years by wind and rain:
the roses on both cheeks had somewhat paled.
What scale could ever weigh their happiness?
She had been gone so long—so many things,
recent or ancient, needed to be told.
Both Van and Quan kept asking this and that,
while Kim looked on, his sorrow turned to joy.

Before the Buddha's altar they knelt down
to offer thanks for Kieu's return to life.
  As sedan-chairs drew up to take them home,
Kieu's father summoned her to come with them.
"I'm nothing but a fallen flower," she said.
"I drank of gall and wormwood half my life.
An exile's destiny was mine, I thought:
to toss upon the waves, beneath the clouds.
I never hoped to see this joyous day,
yet I've survived to meet you all again
and quench the thirst that long has parched my soul.
This shrine lost in the wilds is now my home.
It suits my time and age that I should live
among the grass and trees, far from the world.
I've now acquired a taste for salt and greens.
I've grown to like a nun's brown, humble garb.
And in my heart the fire of greed is out—
why should I struggle still in the Red Dust?
What good is that, a purpose half achieved?
Since I have chosen the monastic path,
I'll try to walk it to the very end.
To her who saved my life I owe a debt
as vast as sea and sky—how can I bear
to cut myself from her and go my way?"
  "Other times, other tides!" old Vuong exclaimed.
"Even religious faith, once in a while,
allows that you obey necessity.
If you devote to Buddha all your life,
who will then take your place and do those tasks
your parents or your lover may require?
The All-High and All-Kind has rescued you—
to his great glory I here pledge a shrine.
We'll ask our Teacher to go there and live."
Heeding her father's word, Kieu had to yield:

135

she took her leave of cloister and old nun.
   The happy group returned to young Kim's home.
For their reunion, they now held a feast.
When liquor had instilled a mellow mood,
Van rose and begged to utter a few thoughts:
"Heaven's design so plans that lovers meet.
Kieu and Kim met—they swore a binding oath.
Over a peaceful earth the waves then swept!
To help my sister honor her sworn vows,
I was called on to wed him she so loved.
Perhaps that had to do with destiny—
amber and mustard seed, magnet and pin!
Besides, could I deny a sister's plea?
It's said that 'when blood flows, the bowels turn soft'.[6]
Day after day, we hoped and prayed for Kieu
with so much love and grief these fifteen years!
But now the mirror cracked is whole again—
Heaven has put her back where she belongs.
She loves him still—her lover is still there.
So is the silver moon they both swore by.
The boughs still have some three or seven plums![7]
The peach tree's still quite fresh![8] It's none too late
to spin and weave the web of marriage bonds."
   When Van was done, Kieu answered in protest:
"Why now retell a tale of long ago?
We once did plight our troth, but since that time
my life has been exposed to wind and rain.
I'd die of shame to talk about the past—
let it go with the stream and down to sea!"
   "A curious way to put it!" Kim cut in.
"Whatever you may feel, your oath remains.
A sacred vow is witnessed by the world—
by earth below, by heaven far above.
Though things may vary and though stars may shift,

in life and death sworn pledges must be kept.
Does fate, which brought you back, oppose our love?
We two are one—why split us in two halves?"

"A happy home where love will reign," said Kieu,
"who does not dream of it? But I believe
a bride must bring her man the purity
of an unopened flower, the perfect shape
of a full moon. Priceless is chastity.
How could I put my dowry on display
under the nuptial torch, before your eyes?
Misfortune struck me—in those days, the flower
became a toy for bees and butterflies.
Swept for so long by wind and drenched by rain,
a rose must fade and wilt, a moon must wane.
What is there left of my two wasted cheeks?
My life is done—how can it be remade?
I can't think of myself and fail to blush—
how dare I soil with the world's dust and dirt
the homespun costume of a virtuous wife?
You bear a constant love for me, I know—
but where to hide my shame by nuptial light?
From this day on I'll bolt my chamber's door—
though I will take no vows, I'll live a nun.
If you still care for what we both once felt,
let's turn it into friendship—let's be friends.
Why speak of marriage and its Red Silk Thread?
It only pains my heart and shames my soul!"

"Such artful dodges words invent!" cried Kim.
"But there's more than one side, more than one truth.
Among those duties falling to her lot,
a woman's chastity means many things,
for there are times of ease and times of stress.
In crisis must all the commands apply?
You sold yourself and proved a daughter's love,

and in this way preserved your chastity.
What dust or dirt could ever sully you?
Heaven has granted us this happy day.
Now from our gate new dawn has swept the mists,
dark clouds have lifted in the sky above;
the faded rose is blooming forth afresh,
the waning moon glows more than at its full!
What is there left to doubt? Why should I play
the thankless role of stranger like that Hsiao⁹
whose wife ignored and snubbed him in the street?"

    Kieu heard Kim through—he argued and he begged,
and both her parents were at one with him.
Outtalked, she could no longer disagree.
She bowed her head and yielded, stifling sighs.

    The family prepared a wedding-feast.
The nuptial candles lighted up the flowers
and set aglow the curtains of red silk.
Before their elders, groom and bride knelt down—
all rites observed, they became man and wife.

    In the bridechamber, both drank from one cup
of tortoise shell. Still shy and ill at ease,
they wistfully recalled their early love.
How young they both had been! A fresh peach bud,
a lotus stem just ready to sprout up.
But fifteen years had intervened since then.
To meet and fall in love, to part and now
to reunite—they felt mixed grief and joy
as deep into the night the moon climbed up.

    The curtains of brocade dropped down their fringe.
Under the light, her two peach-blossom cheeks
gleamed with spring freshness. Lovers met again—
the constant bee, the flower of years long gone.

    "I've done with life, done with myself," said Kieu.
"What further use is there for this spent frame?

I cherished your devotion to the past—
I could not quarrel with the wedding rites.
But how ashamed I felt in my own heart
to lend a brazen front to all that show!
Don't go beyond the outward marks of love—
for then I still can look you in the face.
But if you want to get what they all want,
and from the dirt must glean a whiff of scent
or in late season pluck a wilted bloom,
then we will both present a loathsome scene,
and only hate but no love will be left.
When you make love and I feel only shame,
then crass betrayal's better than such love!
If you must give your clan a rightful heir,
you have my sister—there's no need for me.
Whatever chastity I may have saved,
am I to fling it under trampling feet?
In countless ways you still can prove your love—
why take delight in this flower's faded charms?"

    "By plighted troth we two became as one,"
Kim said. "Then of a sudden we were split
to part like fish in sea from bird in sky.
Through your long exile how I grieved for you!
I suffered so, recalling all our vows.
For love of you I risked life and braved death.
Now you are back—my heart remains the same.
You are still young—a willow in the green.
I thought you still attached to earthly love—
but you show me that not a speck of dust
now tarnishes your mirror any more.
I bow to your decision, and for you
my fond regard increases thousandfold.
If I long searched the sea for the lost pin,
it was for true love's sake, and not because

I sought those pleasures vulgar men so crave.
We're reunited now, inside one home.
Must lovers share one pillow and one mat
to live in concord like zither and harp?"
    Kieu pinned her hair and straightened up her gown.
Then before Kim she fell upon her knees
and knocked her head in gratitude. She cried:
"If my body is ever cleansed of stains,
I'll bless a gentleman, a noble soul!
Now you and I have spoken from our hearts—
there is no truer union than this trust.
A roof, a refuge you have offered me—
my honor lives again as of tonight!"
    She finished with her thanks. Their hands reclasped.
Now he esteemed and loved her all the more.
The candle was replaced, more incense put
in the burner. They filled their cups of jade
and drank more wine to their new happiness.
His old desire for her came flooding back—
he softly asked about the dear lute tune
she once had played. "Those silken notes," she sighed,
"enticed me into my career of woe!
No longer can the harm done be undone.
But I'll obey your wish just one more time."
    Her elfin fingers danced and swept the strings.
As plumes of scentwood smoke curled up and down,
the silk-smooth strains would drift away and back.
Who sang this hymn to life and peace on earth?
Was it a butterfly or Master Chuang?
And who poured forth this rhapsody of love?
The King of Shu or just a cuckoo-bird?
Clear notes like pearls dropped in a moonlit pool!
Warm notes like crystals of new Blue Field jade![10]
    His ears drank in the range of all five tones—

all their accents rejoiced and thrilled his soul.
"The tune's the one of old!" he cried aloud.
"But is the selfsame hand now playing it?
What sounded once so sad now sounds so gay!
Perhaps your soul must cry and laugh by turns—
or does it mean the bitter past is gone
and days of sweet delight have dawned at last?"
"This pleasant little pastime," answered she,
"has earned me nothing but ill luck and grief!
For you this lute just sang its final song.
Henceforth I'll roll its strings and play no more!"

The secrets of two hearts were flowing still
when cocks crowed up the morning in the east.
He talked and made all privy to their pact.
All marveled at her wish and lauded her.
Here was a virtuous woman of high mind,
not one to flirt her way from man to man.

Of love and friendship they fulfilled the claims.
They would forgo one pillow and one mat,
yet they would share the joys of song and verse.
They would drink wine and play a game of chess,
admiring flowers or waiting for the moon.
Their wishes all came true as fate so willed,
and of two lovers marriage made two friends.

As pledged, they built a temple on a hill,
then sent a messenger for the old nun.
When he got there, he found no trace of her.
He knocked the doors—they all were shut and barred.
He saw a weed-grown roof and moss-filled cracks.
She'd gone to gather herbs, he was informed:
the cloud had flown, the crane had fled—whereto?
Kieu paid a loving tribute to the friend
who had long sheltered her: incense and light
were now to burn forever in the shrine.

The twice-blest home enjoyed both weal and wealth.
Kim yearly rose in office, rung by rung.
His Van kept house—a ceaseless round of tasks:
in a stooping tree's shade[11] grew cassia shrubs
and sophoras[12] aplenty in the yard!
In rank and riches who could rival them?
Thus their spring garden throve to leave behind
their name and fame for all ages to come.

All things are fixed by Heaven, first and last.
Heaven appoints each creature to a place.
If we are marked for grief, we'll come to grief.
We'll sit on high when destined for high seats.
And Heaven with an even hand will give
talent to some, to others happiness.
In talent take no overweening pride—
great talent and misfortune make a pair.[13]
A Karma each of us has to live out:
let's stop decrying Heaven's quirks and whims.
Within us each there lies the root of good:
the heart means more than all talents on earth.

May these crude words, culled and strung one by one,
beguile an hour or two of your long night.

Notes

I

1   *the sea now rolls where mulberry-fields grew*] A passage in
    the Chinese collection entitled *Stories of Gods and Fai-
    ries (Shen Hsien Chuan)* reads: "Every thirty years, the
    vast sea turns into mulberry-fields and mulberry-fields
    turn into the vast sea." Hence, the Vietnamese phrase
    'sea and mulberry' *(be dau)* refers in elliptical form to
    some upheaval either in nature or in the affairs of men.

2   *Chia-ch'ing*] the reign title of the Ming emperor Shih-
    tsung who ruled China from 1522 to 1566.

3   *both Capitals*] Ming China had two capitals: Peking (the
    Northern Capital) and Nanking (the Southern Capital).
    Kieu's family lived in Peking—this fact will not be men-
    tioned in the poem until much later.

4   *A glance or two from her, and cities rocked!*] a paraphrase
    of two lines from a song by Li Yen-nien who founded the
    Music Department *(Yüeh-fu)* under the Han dynasty.

5   *all five tones*] The traditional Chinese scale has five tones: *kung* (C), *shang* (D), *chiao* (E), *chih* (G), and *yü* (A).

6   *the lute*] the *p'i-p'a*, a four-stringed, pear-shaped guitar, which looks rather like the European lute.

7   *Ai Chang*] short for Ai Ju-chang, the most famous Han lutanist.

8   *that time when maidens pinned their hair*] In old China, girls ritually pinned up their hair, when they reached the age of fifteen, as a sign that they were ready for marriage.

9   *the Eastern wall*] In the *Mencius*, one of *The Four Books* of Confucianism, there is censure of a certain fellow who "climbed over the wall of neighbors to the east and tried to seduce their daughter." A Chinese equivalent of the wall under Juliet's balcony, the "Eastern wall" has become the symbol of an illicit love tryst.

10   *the Feast of Light*] Ch'ing-ming (Pure and Bright), a spring festival in China, when people put graves in order and make offerings to the dead.

11   *the pin had snapped in two, the pitcher sunk*] Chinese metaphors for the death of one's wife or ladylove.

12   *the Yellow Springs*] the nether world—also known as the Nine Springs.

13   *four lines of cut-off verse*] a *chüeh-chü* (cut-off lines) quatrain invented by T'ang poets to express intense feelings in the most compact form.

14   *an old-style poem*] a *ku-shih* poem not subject to length, rhyme and tone restrictions and therefore a better medium than a regulated *(lü-shih)* poem for expressing a flood of feelings.

15   *two beauties locked in a Bronze Sparrow Tower*] In the Three Kingdoms period of Chinese history, Ts'ao Ts'ao (155–220) of Wei vowed to defeat the state of Wu and capture the two beautiful Ch'iao sisters for the harem of

his palace, the Bronze Sparrow Tower, in Honan. But a favorable wind enabled Chou Yü, the young military commander of Wu, to destroy Ts'ao's fleet in 208 at a spot on the Yangtze called the Red Cliff. In a well-known quatrain, the T'ang poet Tu Mu (803–852) wrote: *Had the East wind not helped young Chou, the Bronze Sparrow/ would have locked up two beauties in their spring.*

16 *two golden lotus blooms*] bound feet of a beautiful woman. When his concubine, P'an Fei, danced on a floor decorated with golden lotus flowers, the Marquis of Tung-hun, sixth ruler of the Southern Ch'i dynasty (479–501), said: "At every step a lotus grows!" Foot-binding for women was a Chinese custom never adopted in Vietnam.

17 *the Peach Blossom Source*] "Peach Blossom Source," a prose piece written by the Chinese poet-recluse T'ao Ch'ien (365–427), tells of a fisherman from Wu-ling who lost his way and wandered into an arcadia through a small opening in the side of a hill, near where peach blossoms were in bloom. After he returned to the world and reported his discovery, no one was able to find that happy land again.

18 *the League Chief*] the head of the League of Sorrow whose members are women of beauty and talent who are doomed by fate. Their names appear in the Book of the Damned.

19 *tears rain down on your pear-blossom face*] That is how the T'ang poet Po Chü-yi (772–846) describes the beautiful Yang Kuei-fei in tears in "A Song of Unending Sorrow."

20 *the Blue Bridge*] According to Chinese Taoist lore, a T'ang man met a nymph near the Blue Bridge (Lan-ch'iao) in Lan-t'ien, Shensi, and eventually married her, attaining

immortality himself. The "Blue Bridge" has come to mean a place where one encounters a beautiful girl whom one is to wed.

21 *No stream to float the Crimson Leaf of love!*] A T'ang man found a crimson leaf on a stream flowing out of the Imperial Palace—it carried a poem by a member of the imperial harem. He wrote a poem in reply on another leaf and floated it into the palace on the stream; by chance, the girl found it. Later, she was discharged from the harem. The two met, fell in love and married only to discover that they had written to each other before.

22 *No passage for the bluebird to bear news!*] The Queen Mother of the West (Hsi Wang Mu), the highest goddess in the Chinese Taoist pantheon, used two bluebirds as messengers. In romantic literature, the bluebird is the harbinger of love.

23 *a well-named porch—Kingfisher View*] 'Thuy' in 'Thuy Kieu' means kingfisher.

24 *golden*] 'Kim' in 'Kim Trong' means gold.

25 *The pearl wants to go back—but where's Ho-p'u?*] Ho-p'u in Chiao-chou (present-day North Vietnam, which was then part of the Chinese empire) was once famous for its pearl fisheries. But when reckless exploitation depleted the supply of pearls people claimed that the pearls had fled. Then a wise governor was appointed, and he took measures to revive the pearl fisheries. When they began to produce again, people said the pearls were coming back. Thus, "a pearl going back to Ho-p'u" is something being returned to where it belongs, to its rightful owner.

26 *I've hugged my forlorn hope like that poor lad/ who hugged a pillar waiting for his love.*] Wei Sheng, waiting for a tryst with his beloved, who never came, stubbornly

stayed under a bridge, hugging a pillar, until he drowned in the rising tide.

27   *the Red Thread of marriage*] According to Chinese folklore, the Wedlock God (or Old Man of the Moon) picks a man and a woman and binds them together with a red thread.

28   *her sunflower fan—the flower of constancy*] The sunflower, which always turns to the sun (the *yang,* or male, principle), is a symbol of women's submission and faithfulness to their husbands, according to Confucian ethics.

29   *The Hsiang River ran dry—a trickle now:/ he waited at the source, she at the mouth.*] The Hsiang River stands for lovelorn grief because, according to Chinese tradition, it was on its bank that the two sisters O-huang and Nü-ying wasted away mourning and pining for their common husband, the sage-king Shun. But the direct inspiration for these two lines comes from an old Chinese song: *He stays at the source of the Hsiang./ She stays at the mouth of the Hsiang./ Unseeing, both yearn for each other./ Both drink the water of the Hsiang.*

30   *Pan and Hsieh*] Pan Chao under the Han and Hsieh Tao-yün under the Chin were accomplished women of letters.

31   *You'll cross the Golden Portal and wear jade.*] Scholar-officials wore jade insignia as badges of rank. The Golden Portal was the entrance for high court ministers under Emperor Han Wu-ti.

32   *Mount Chia*] The Nymph of Love lived on Mount Chia, where she made clouds by day and rain by night—clouds and rain being a Chinese metaphor for sexual intercourse.

33   *Mount Shen*] an abode of the gods.

34   *a game of moon and flowers*] erotic love as something

transient, not expected to last, like the moon that wanes and flowers that fade. A plighted troth leading to marriage and the perpetuation of the family must be engraved on "stone and bronze."

35   *Chung Tzu-ch'i*] He was the only person who fully appreciated Po Ya's lute-playing. After Chung died, Po broke the strings of his lute and played no more.

36   *moon-shaped lute*] the *yüeh-ch'in*, or four-stringed moon-shaped guitar.

37   *Han and Ch'u*] Liu Pang of Han and Hsiang Yü of Ch'u fought each other for the domination of China—Liu triumphed and founded the Han dynasty in 206 B.C.

38   *The Ssu-ma tune,* A Phoenix Seeks His Mate] The Han writer Ssu-ma Hsiang-ju (179–117 B.C.) played *A Phoenix Seeks His Mate* on the lute and captured the heart of a young widow, Cho Wen-chün: she eloped with him against her father's wishes.

39   *Hsi K'ang's masterpiece,* Kuang-ling] In the Three Kingdoms period of Chinese history, Hsi K'ang (223–262) was a musician belonging to a group of Taoist anarchists known as the Seven Sages of the Bamboo Grove. He was noted for his playing of a tune called *Kuang-ling*.

40   *Chao-chün*] To appease the Tartar Khan who wanted a Chinese wife, Emperor Han Yüan-ti sent him one of his concubines, Wang Chao-chün. This incident is often treated in Chinese literature—it is the subject of a play by Ma Chih-yüan in the thirteenth century: *Autumn in the Palace of Han* (translated by Donald Keene and available in Cyril Birch, *Anthology of Chinese Literature*, Grove Press, Inc., New York, 1965).

41   *those mulberry-groves on the P'u River banks*] In the ancient state of Wei (now eastern Honan and southern Hopei), mulberry-groves along the P'u River served as

trysting places for lovers and acquired a notorious reputation.

42 *Ts'ui and Chang*] The two most famous lovers in Chinese literature, Ts'ui Ying-ying and Scholar Chang are the heroine and hero of a probably semi-autobiographical story in prose by the T'ang poet Yüan Chen (779–831). Provided with a happy ending, it was turned by Wang Shih-fu (active at the end of the thirteenth and beginning of the fourteenth centuries) into a dramatic masterpiece, *Hsi-hsiang chi*. Both the play and the original tale can be found in S. I. Hsiung, tr., *The Romance of the Western Chamber*, Columbia Universtiy Press, New York, 1968. In the nineteenth century, Nguyen Le Quang adapted the play into a 1,744-line poem in Vietnamese.

43 *wing to wing and limb to limb they lay*] an allusion to the love affair between Emperor Ming-huang and Lady Yang (Yang Kuei-fei) as described by Po Chü-yi in "A Song of Unending Sorrow."

44 *cast the shuttle to resist*] To drive away an unwanted suitor who bothered her while she was working at the loom, a girl hurled the shuttle at him, breaking his teeth.

II

1 *Liao-yang*] a county in Manchuria.

2 *No one but you shall ever be my man/ and hear me play my lute aboard his boat*] In "A Ballad of the Lute" *(P'i-p'a hsing)*, the T'ang poet Po Chü-yi tells of his chance meeting with a courtesan who, once celebrated for her looks and lute-playing in the capital of Ch'ang-an, was now the lonely wife of an often absent tea-merchant and

played the lute all by herself on her houseboat. Playwrights have elaborated this simple incident into a love story involving Po himself as a central figure: he is supposed to have in Ch'ang-an a passionate affair with the courtesan, who swears eternal love to him but eventually lets herself be sold to the tea-merchant. Based on this fictitious episode, "to carry one's lute and go aboard another man's boat" means, for a woman, to play her lover false and leave him for somebody else.

3 *From spring a leaf of grass receives its green . . .*] This comes from two lines in "A Wanderer's Song" by the T'ang poet Meng Chiao (751–814): *Who says that a son's heart, an inch of grass,/ can ever full requite the warmth of spring?* Although Meng's poem is about a man's grateful remembrance of his mother, spring as a metaphor usually refers to the father: one owes one's life to him even as grass owes its growth to the three warm months of spring.

4 *Scholar Ma—of the Imperial University*] 'Giam-sinh' (Chin. *Chien-sheng*) in 'Ma Giam-sinh' means someone who is or used to be a student at the Imperial University or National College (Chin. *Kuo-tzu-chien*).

5 *she'll toss the ball into some worthy hands*] According to tradition, Emperor Han Wu-ti's daughter threw down a ball from her tower to a group of suitors gathered below: the one who caught the ball won her hand.

6 *Ying*] During the Han dynasty, T'i-ying dared to petition the Emperor and saved her father from an unjust accusation.

7 *Li*] According to a T'ang story, a girl named Li Chi wanted to earn money for her poor parents: she sold herself to be used as a human sacrifice to a snake demon. She slew the monster and married the King of Yüeh.

8   *the Old Man of the Moon*] the Wedlock God who binds
    men and women with a red thread.

9   *the Nine Springs*] the nether world—also known as the
    Yellow Springs.

10 *From amber who has torn the mustard seed*] By friction
    amber becomes strongly electric and attracts mustard
    seeds—this phenomenon serves as a metaphor for
    mutual affinity leading to love and marriage.

11 *the East wind*] the wind that blows in spring and therefore
    favors love.

12 *she swapped her sawdust for his bitter melon*] The Viet-
    namese proverbial phrase 'sawdust and bitter melon'
    (mat cua muop dang) refers to a pair of well-matched
    swindlers. Although of rather uncertain origin, it is some-
    times plausibly explained as follows: a hawker who
    palmed off sawdust *(mat cua)* for rice bran on unsuspect-
    ing customers came across another who peddled bitter
    melons *(muop dang)* for cucumbers—they traded their
    goods, duping each other.

13 *He waves the flag who holds it in his hand!*] A Vietnamese
    proverb says: *Whoever holds a flag in his hand waves it
    (Co vao tay ai, nguoi ay phat).*

III

1   *Lin-tzu*] Under the Ming dynasty, it was a *hsien* in Shan-
    tung Province.

2   *Ch'ien-t'ang River*] a river in Chekiang Province.

3   *hsi yüeh*] The two Chinese characters 昔 越 can be
    broken down into five others, 廿 一 日 戌 走 *(nien
    i jih hsü tsou)*, which mean: "Flee on the twenty-first

day, hour of the Dog." Hour of the Dog: between 7 and 9 P.M.

4 *I will knot grass*] To 'knot grass' *(ket co,* Chin. *chieh ts'ao)* is to repay an act of kindness. The expression comes from the following Chinese story. On his deathbed, Wei Wu-tzu, a great officer of the state of Chin in the sixth century B.C., gave the order that when he died his child-less concubine should be buried with him. His son Wei K'o, disobeying the paternal injunction, let her live. Later, in a battle, he captured a Ch'in warrior, the famous Tu Hui, with the help of an old man who tripped up Tu Hui with knots of grass. That night, the old man appeared to Wei K'o in a dream and said that he was the father of the concubine whose life had been spared.

5 *I will fetch the jade rings*] To 'fetch the jade rings' (*ngam vanh,* Chin. *hsien huan,* literally: to 'carry rings in the mouth or beak') is another expression of gratitude. Yang Pao, a young Han boy, saved a wounded yellow bird from ants and took good care of it until it grew strong enough to fly away. That night, the bird came back as a boy dressed in yellow and bearing as gifts four white jade rings or badges of high office. Indeed, four generations of Yang's descendants rose to important posts in government.

6 *An eel ought not to mind soiling its head.*] This is a Vietnamese proverb with the following variant: *Would an eel mind soiling its eyes?*—which means: a person who has fallen quite low is ready to do anything, however disgraceful.

7 *the feint of the swordsman in flight*] As a tactic in swordsmanship, one pretends to flee and lets one's opponent come close enough, then one suddenly turns around and attacks him when he least expects it.

8 *Birds thronged the branch, winds stirred the leaves.*] This is

a brief paraphrase of two lines from a poem by Hsüeh T'ao (767?–831), a famous T'ang courtesan: *The branch greets birds from south and north./ The leaves sway back and forth with winds.*

9 *She'd speed/ Sung Yü at dawn, wait for Ch'ang-ch'ing at dusk.*] Sung Yü, a Ch'u poet of the third century B.C., and Ch'ang-ch'ing (or Ssu-ma Hsiang-ju), a Han poet (179–117 B.C.), were notorious womanizers, according to tradition.

10 *the Nine Great Debts*] the nine laborious tasks which parents have performed for their children's sake: birth, feeding, upbringing, etc., and which demand requital by acts of filial piety, according to a song ("Lu o") in *The Book of Odes.*

11 *Willow on Chang Terrace*] Under the T'ang dynasty, Miss Willow was a courtesan living in the capital of Ch'ang-an, on a street named Chang Terrace. Han Hsiu, her lover, had to leave her and take up a far-away post. From there he wrote her a poem with these lines: *O Chang Terrace Willow, Chang Terrace Willow!/ Are you still fresh and green as you were once?* When he came back, she was gone—she had been abducted by a Tartar general.

12 *Time fled on moon-hare's feet and sun-crow's wings.*] Chinese mythology claims that there is a white hare on the moon and a golden crow on the sun.

IV

1 *a T'ang poem*] a *lü-shih* (regulated verse) poem, composed in strict accordance with rules laid down under the T'ang dynasty (618–907), which is generally regarded as the Golden Age of Chinese poetry.

2 *wu-t'ung*] the national tree of China *(Sterculia platani-folia)*, which somewhat resembles the plane tree and is associated with autumn in literature.

3 *my fingers have dipped in indigo*] Indigo is a fast dye, not easy to wash or scrub away—hence, the Vietnamese proverbial phrase, *One's hands have dipped in indigo (Tay da nhung cham)*, meaning that one has made some mistake difficult or impossible to correct.

4 *Chou and Ch'en*] In ancient China, Chou and Ch'en were the only two clans making up a certain village, and they intermarried.

5 *The ant's inside the cup—where could it crawl?*] "The ant is crawling on the rim of the cup" *(Kien bo mieng chen)* is a Vietnamese proverb about someone in a perilous situation from which there is no escape.

6 *a homely diet of fish grass and tench*] On an autumn day Chang Han, a high official under the Chin dynasty, missed the taste of fish grass *(ch'un)* and tench *(hsü)*, common dishes of his native countryside—thereupon he resigned and went back home. Unlike Chang Han, however, young Thuc got tired of home cooking and was dreaming of more exotic fare.

7 *Ch'ang-o*] According to Chinese mythology, Ch'ang-o stole the pill of immortality from her husband, ate it and fled to the moon where she has been living alone ever since.

8 *the Three Isles*] the Islands of Bliss in the Eastern Sea, according to Taoist lore.

9 *the Gate of the Void*] the door to nirvana—a general name for Buddhism.

10 *Kuan-yin*] the Buddhist Goddess of Mercy, Listener to the World's Cries.

11 *lotus and bo tree*] Both are central symbols of Buddhism. The lotus, growing in mud and not smelling of mud,

represents purity in an impure world. A bo tree (or pipal, *Ficus religiosa*) was the tree under which Sakyamuni attained enlightenment and became Buddha.

12 *the Three Pledges*] Upon becoming a monk or nun, a Buddhist pledges himself or herself to the Three Precious Ones: Buddha, Dharma (or the Law), and Sangha (or the Order).

13 *the Five Commands*] Binding on Buddhist laity, male and female, as well as on monks and nuns, there are five commandments against killing, stealing, lewdness, lying, and the drinking of alcohol.

14 *the Purple Grove*] Kuan-yin stayed at a grove of purple bamboos, according to Buddhist tradition.

15 *the Red Dust*] the world of mundane concerns dominated by greed and lust.

16 *Kuan-yin's willow branch*] Kuan-yin is often represented with a willow branch in her hand, scattering drops of mercy on a suffering world.

17 *Dhyana*] meditation or contemplation, therefore Buddhism in general, or especially the Ch'an (meditative, intuitional) school founded in China by Bodhidharma, the twenty-eighth patriarch.

18 *Lan-t'ing*] 'Orchid Pavilion,' a location in the mountains near Shao-hsing in Chekiang. Wang Hsi-chih (321–379), China's most celebrated calligrapher, held a party there on a spring day, during which he produced his best work.

V

1 *Sign of Peach Blossom*] the astrological sign under which courtesans are born.

2 *Great Potter's Wheel*] the Creator as shaper of human destinies.

3 *A tiger's beard, a jaw like swallow's beak,/ brows thick as silkworms—tough and fierce, his looks*] the portrait of a soldier destined for greatness, in accordance with Chinese physiognomy.

4 *none of them earned grace in your clear eyes*] This is an allusion to Juan Chi (210–263), the most eccentric member of a group known as the Seven Sages of the Bamboo Grove during the Three Kingdoms period of Chinese history. He refused to see people he disliked, showing them the whites of his eyes, and reserved his clear pupils only for the chosen few.

5 *It calls to mind that verse on Prince P'ing-yüan.*] Prince P'ing-yüan, of the kingdom of Chao in the Warring States period of Chinese history, was celebrated for his hospitality and generosity—he liked to take people under his wing. Two lines from a T'ang poem read: *I know not whom to give my heart and soul./ It makes me long for Prince P'ing-yüan of old.* When Kieu said: *"But oh, where shall I ever find the one/ to whom I can entrust my heart and soul?,"* she paraphrased that poem, implying that she was looking for a Prince P'ing-yüan. Tu Hai recognized the poem, understood the hint, and was highly pleased with being cast by Kieu in the role of a magnanimous protector.

6 *Chin-yang*] where the rebel Li Yüan ascended the throne in 618 as T'ang Kao-tsu, the founder of the great T'ang dynasty, which lasted until 907.

7 *Thief and old woman meet.*] *Ke cap ba gia gap nhau* is a Vietnamese folk saying about two well-matched opponents. It must have come from some folk tale now lost.

8 *Han Hsin*] When he was still a poor, hungry fisherman,

Han Hsin was befriended by an old washerwoman who gave him a bowl of rice. Later, thanks to his military genius, he helped Liu Pang triumph over Hsiang Yü and mount the throne in 206 B.C. as Emperor Han Kao-tsu, the founder of the Han dynasty. Now the most prestigious general of the empire, Han Hsin repaid the old washerwoman's bowl of rice with gold. That grateful man, however, fell victim to political ingratitude: suspected of actual or potential treason, he was degraded and put to death by Emperor Han Kao-tsu.

9   *the Wayward River*] So called because it often shifts its course, the Wayward *(Wu-ting)* River is a tributary of the Yellow River, flowing from Suiyüan in Inner Mongolia to Shensi. It was the site of many bloody battles between the Chinese and the Tartars. Ch'en T'ao, a T'ang poet of the ninth century, wrote this quatrain called "Lung-hsi Song": *They pledged their lives to sweep the Huns away./ Five thousand braves in furs bit Tartar dust./ Pity their bones which rim the Wayward River./ As men, they haunt their women's dreams in spring.*

10   *Huang Ch'ao*] An unsuccessful scholar, he led his fellow rebels to capture Ch'ang-an in 881, proclaimed himself Emperor, but was soon defeated and slain in 884. His revolt dealt the T'ang dynasty a blow from which it was not to recover.

11   *My heartstrings broke just like Hsiao Lin's lute strings.*] Hsiao Lin, concubine of the king of Ch'i (a feudal state which lasted from 1122 to 265 B.C.), was forced to marry another man. As she was playing the lute one day, its strings broke. She was moved to compose a poem with the following lines: *You want to know how my poor heartstrings snapped?/ Look at the strings of the lute on my pillow.*

VI

1   *Only the peach blossoms of yesteryear/ were flirting still
with the frolic East wind.*] The T'ang poet Ts'ui Hu
wrote this quatrain entitled "Inscribed at a Place Visited
Once Before": *A year ago today, within this gate,/ her
face and peach blossoms both blushed alike./ I do not
know where to look for her face./ Peach blossoms,
though, still smile at the East wind.*

2   *The planks of wood already have been nailed into a boat.*]
This is a Vietnamese proverb *(Van da dong thuyen)*
expressing quiet acceptance of some irrevocable situation.

3   *Chin-shih*] a scholar who passed the highest examinations
for a degree equivalent to the modern doctorate and
normally required for appointment to office.

4   *the Highroad of Blue Clouds*] an official career for *Chin-
shih* graduates.

5   *the errant bird's lost soul*] After the daughter of Emperor
Yen (Yen-ti) drowned in the sea, her unhappy soul
turned into a *ching-wei* bird which flew about picking
stones and pebbles and throwing them into the sea in a
vain attempt to fill it up.

6   *When blood flows, the bowels turn soft.*] This is a Vietnamese proverb *(Mau chay ruot mem)* about family soli-
darity: when a member of the family gets hurt, the other
members get hurt and can't remain unconcerned about
his or her trouble.

7   *The boughs still have some three or seven plums!*] Implying
that Kieu is not yet too old for marriage, this is an
allusion to a courtship song in *The Book of Odes: Down
fall the plums—/ but there are seven left./ Good sirs*

who're courting me,/ choose quick a lucky day./ Down fall the plums—/ but there are three left still./ Good sirs who're courting me,/ make up your mind right now./ Down fall the plums—/a basket gathers them./ Good sirs who're courting me,/ speak up while there's still time.

8 *The peach tree's still quite fresh!*] This is also a reference to *The Book of Odes*, which has this marriage song: *How fresh, the young peach tree!/ How bright its blossoms shine!/ The lass follows her spouse./ She'll run their house and home./ How fresh, the young peach tree!/ How many fruits it bears!/ The lass follows her spouse./ She'll run their home and house./ How fresh, the young peach tree!/ How lush and green, its leaves!/ The lass follows her spouse./ She'll rule their maids and men.*

9 *the thankless role of stranger like that Hsiao*] Hsiao's wife, Lu-chu ('Green Pearl'), was abducted and offered as a concubine to a powerful official. Since then, she no longer recognized her husband and looked away when she saw him in the street.

10 *Who sang this hymn . . . Blue Field jade!*] This whole passage is a paraphrase of the four middle lines from "The Ornamented Zither," the best known, and least understood, poem by the T'ang poet Li Shang-yin (813–858). The mention of a butterfly and Master Chuang (or Chuang-tzu) alludes to a passage in the *Chuang Tzu*, a Taoist classic: "Once upon a time, Chuang Chou [i.e., Chuang-tzu] dreamed that he was a butterfly, fluttering to and fro and enjoying itself. It did not know that it was Chuang Chou. Suddenly he awoke and was Chuang Chou again. But he did not know whether he was Chuang Chou who had dreamed that he was a butterfly, or whether he was a butterfly dreaming that it was Chuang Chou." Wang-ti, the king of Shu, carried on a love affair with the wife of his minister until he was

discovered: he fled into exile and died, turning into a cuckoo or nightjar. Mount Lan-t'ien ('Blue Field') in Shensi is renowned for its jade.

11 *in a stooping tree's shade*] The 'stooping tree,' a phrase found in *The Book of Odes,* usually designates the first-rank wife who supports and protects the concubines as 'clinging vines.' Although the expression can apply to Kieu, it probably refers here to Van as a mother taking good care of her many children.

12 *cassia shrubs and sophoras*] These plants and trees stand for sons destined to succeed as scholars and officials.

13 *great talent and misfortune make a pair*] The words for 'talent' *(tài,* Chin. *ts'ai)* and 'misfortune' *(tai,* Chin. *tsai)* rhyme in Vietnamese and Chinese.

A Short Bibliography
in English and French

I. Vietnamese literature and history

Durand, Maurice, and Nguyen Tran Huan. *Introduction à la Littérature Vietnamienne*. Paris: G. P. Maisonneuve et Larose, 1969.

Le Thanh Khoi. *Le Viet-Nam, Histoire et Civilisation*. Paris: Les Éditions de Minuit, 1955.

Marr, David G. *Vietnamese Anticolonialism*. Berkeley: University of California Press, 1971.

Truong Buu Lam. *Patterns of Vietnamese Response to Foreign Intervention, 1858–1900*. Monograph Series No. 11. New Haven: Southeast Asia Studies, Yale University, 1967.

Woodside, Alexander B. *Vietnam and the Chinese Model*. Cambridge, Mass.: Harvard University Press, 1971.

II. Nguyen Du and *The Tale of Kieu*

apRoberts, Ruth. "Vietnamese Classic," *Literature East and West*, December 1969. Austin, Texas.

Durand, Maurice, ed. *Mélanges sur Nguyen Du*. Paris: École Française d'Extrême-Orient, 1966.

Vietnamese Studies, April 1965. Hanoi: Foreign Languages Publishing House.

III. French translations of *The Tale of Kieu*

Crayssac, René. *Kim Van Kieou*. Hanoi: Le Van Tan, 1926. [Alexandrine verse.]

Nguyen Khac Vien. *Kieu*. Hanoi: Éditions en Langues Étrangères, 1965. [Free verse.]

Nguyen Van Vinh. *Kim Van Kieu*. Hanoi: Éditions Alexandre de Rhodes, 1942. [Prose.]

Xuan Phuc and Xuan Viet. *Kim Van Kieu*. Paris: Gallimard, 1961. [Prose.]

About the Translator

HUYNH SANH THONG was born in 1926 in Hoc-mon, Gia-dinh Province, Vietnam. He was educated at the Lycée Truong Vinh Ky in Saigon, at Ohio University in Athens, Ohio, and at Cornell University in Ithaca, New York. He is a member of Phi Beta Kappa. He has spent his adult life in the United States and taught Vietnamese at various universities, including Yale. At present he is doing research under the auspices of the Vietnam Studies Coordinating Group of the Association for Asian Studies. As an avocation he translates poetry into English and is completing an anthology of T'ang verse. He and his wife, Yen, live in Hamden, Connecticut, with their three children: Thi, Thanh, and Tung.

02   304